FRENCH
COUNTRY
KITCHENS

FRENCH COUNTRY KITCHENS

LINDA DANNENBERG

PHOTOGRAPHS BY GUY BOUCHET

CLARKSON POTTER/PUBLISHERS
NEW YORK

Preceding pages, left In a Left Bank Paris kitchen decorated by Marie-Dominique de Montmaurin, eighteenth-century Delft tiles serve as a backdrop for a set of vintage copper pots.

Opposite Eighteenth-century heart-shaped molds from the collection of Philippe Irrmann.

Fabrics
Rayure "Marquis de Pierre," Bleu (endpapers); "Mennecy," Moutarde (pages 18–19); "Louvois," Vert Mousse (pages 70–71); "Robinson," Bleu (pages 112–113); "Figueras," Acajou (pages 152–153); "Sénanque," Rose Ancien (pages 182–183). All from Pierre Frey and reproduced with their kind permission.

Library of Congress Cataloging-in-Publication Data
Dannenberg, Linda.
    French country kitchens / by Linda Dannenberg ; photographs by Guy Bouchet.
    1. Kitchens. 2. Interior decoration—France. I. Title.
NK2117.K5D36 2008
747.7'97—dc22   2007048072

978-0-307-35272-9

Printed in China

Design by Maggie Hinders

10 9 8 7 6 5 4 3 2 1

First Edition

To Steve and Ben, who share my kitchen

and fill it with so much joy

ACKNOWLEDGMENTS

DURING the many months I spent in France seeking out iconic, imaginative, and unique kitchens, I thought every day about how privileged I was to be producing this book. It was work, of course, but *quelle joie*! One day I would be driving along an obscure country lane in the Île-de-France to an isolated farmhouse with delightful décor, on another perhaps searching for kitchen collectibles at a bustling village flea market in the Vaucluse. And at the end of so many days, I found myself dining among friends and colleagues in the Alpilles around a table laden with memorable food and wine. These pages reflect the generosity, cooperation, conviviality, friendship, and enthusiastic involvement of many people, including Ghyslaine Béguin, Brigitte Benoît-Vernin, Nathalie Besnard, Michel Biehn, Vincent Boeuf, Lucille and Jacques Bons, Marie-Colette and Jean-Michel Borgeaud, Hugues Bosc, Françoise and Jean-Pierre Boudin-Conte, Dr. Tandra Cadigan, Bruno Carles, Éric Chailloux, Dominique Cornwell, Édith de Ménibus, Marie-Dominique de Montmaurin, Hannelore and Renato de Paolis, Marie-Catherine Dupuy, Philippe Eckert, Mr. and Mrs. Hans-Georg Feick, Olivier Fouret, Danielle and Jean-Claude Gandon, Nono Girard, Françoise and Patrick Hontebeyrie, Philippe Irrmann, Daniel Léonhardt, Catherine Ligeard, Isabelle and Édouard Loubet, Pierre Mesguich, Bernard and Véronique Murat, Mechtild and Jochen Neynaber, Kathy and Lloyd Otterman, Martine Ouvrard, Franca Pannier, Carole Peck and Bernard Jarrier, Marie-José Pommereau, Estelle Réale, Michel Rostang, Sharyl and Paul Rupert, Martin Stein, Aline and Erwin Steinbach, Gertjan van der Hoest, Maria-Pia Varnier, Esther Carliner Viros, Caroline Vogelsang, Stanley and Lorenzo Weisman, and Patricia and Walter Wells. I am so grateful to them all.

I am extremely grateful to Lorraine Frey for inviting me to visit the extraordinary fabric archives of the Pierre Frey headquarters in Paris, and for kindly allowing us to reproduce several gorgeous Pierre Frey fabrics in these pages. My warm thanks as well to Patrick Frey in Paris, and to Pierre Frey and Kim Huebner for their help in the New York Pierre Frey showroom.

A special thanks to the talented Hélène Lafforgue, stylist and journalist extraordinaire, who worked on several locations in this book.

It is also a privilege to work with the terrific team of publishers, editors, and designers at Clarkson Potter. They have been an important part of my life for more than twenty years. My deep appreciation to my longtime friend and esteemed publisher, Lauren Shakely; my gifted and patient editor, Pam Krauss, whose expertise smoothly guided this long-dreamed-about project from proposal to beautiful book; Maggie Hinders, whose inspired design reflects the charm and captivating style of French country; creative director Marysarah Quinn and art director Jane Treuhaft; Peggy Paul; and Sibylle Kazeroid.

Finally, I would like to express my heartfelt thanks and affection to my treasured friend and agent of two decades, Gayle Benderoff, whose clear-sighted guidance and unwavering support on every book project is invaluable.

Late-nineteenth- and early-twentieth-century enamelware decks the shelves of Au Petit Bonheur La Chance in Paris.

Contents

INTRODUCTION:
AT HOME IN THE KITCHEN

WHEN I THINK BACK on all the homes I've visited in the French countryside—and I've visited hundreds over the last twenty-five years—it is almost always the kitchens I remember most clearly and recall with the most affection. This is likely because the kitchen is always the room in which I end up spending most of my time in a French home, chatting over coffee, sipping an aperitif, helping with meal preparations, and sharing a joyous dinner, be it an omelette or a feast, with friends and new acquaintances.

It is there at the table that we linger over little stemmed glasses of Armagnac or eau-de-vie discussing life's mysteries, or friends' affairs, long into the night. After creating five books on French country style that feature homes throughout France, I decided it was time to do a book exclusively on the kitchen, my favorite room. I visited more than two hundred kitchens, each unique, and more

than sixty-five of them are presented in these pages. Photographer Guy Bouchet and I were always received with memorable warmth and generosity, often being invited to stay for lunch or dinner as honored guests.

The heart and soul of the French country home—and the source of France's legendary *art de vivre*—is the kitchen. It is a room unlike any other, one that inspires conviviality and manifests the Gallic passion for good food. Many of the French kitchens I've seen are the stuff of dreams, full of style, charm, and whimsy, whether they are tiny and simple as can be or grandly scaled and lavishly furnished by a top decorator. From rustic to opulent, each of these kitchens possesses its own personality and purpose.

The most simple might have a modest piece of linen or muslin concealing the contents of the cabinets, salvaged cement tile on the floor, and an electric stove dating from the 1960s; the most lavish might have custom-designed tiles created by Gilles Delfino of Cannes, cabinets sheltered behind

Rich tones of green, yellow, and terra-cotta warm a classic country kitchen in an eighteenth-century Provençal home near Fontvielle.

eighteenth-century armoire doors, and a gorgeous, enameled, brass-fitted La Cornue stove. Decorative elements in a modest kitchen might include a single sunflower in an old apothecary bottle; in the most elegant, one might find a precious eighteenth-century still life, its frame gilded in eighteen-karat gold. No kitchen better represents the harmony of form, function, regional style, art, tradition, and familial warmth than the French country kitchen. The best comprise a fine use of colors, modern and vintage elements and equipment, imaginative yet functional storage, and practical yet stylish lighting.

When I reflect on the French country kitchen, and try to pinpoint what general characteristics contribute to its distinction, several tendencies and design philosophies spring to mind. One is the low incidence of built-in cabinetry. Instead, there are always several pieces of freestanding furniture clustered around the sink and the stove: an armoire, small chests, a couple of tables, a wall-hung étagère, and sometimes a piece of furniture for food storage called a *garde-manger* (literally, "keep to eat"). The *garde-manger* resembles an armoire but is equipped with open grillwork or screened-in doors and sides to aerate cooling tarts and jams, and to store bread, dried sausages, and sometimes cheese. Under-the-counter storage may be camouflaged by gaily patterned curtains rather than a cabinet door.

In some kitchens, owners decide to sacrifice practicality and efficiency for personality and tradition, opting for the same kind of kitchen their grandparents had, with lots of individual pieces of furniture but not much counter space or dedicated work area. To preserve an old-fashioned look and atmosphere, the owners are ready to forgo built-ins that typically include broad, usable countertops. In these cases, a sturdy dining table usually does double duty as an island-like food prep station. Where there is built-in shelving, it is very often open rather than hidden behind doors, in order to display heirloom tureens, crystal, serving platters, vases, and small collectibles.

Because the world of design is not static, however, and changes in perception and desire are inevitable, the French country kitchen will eventually evolve in favor of modern style and convenience, judging from the burgeoning number of *cuisinistes*, specialized kitchen design firms, throughout France. The *cuisinistes* have a penchant for built-in cabinetry, designer islands, high-tech appliances, and lots of counter space, a style of kitchen the French call *une cuisine américaine*. Practicality may one day trump tradition.

Many kitchens in the French countryside boast a functioning fireplace, an important element for many families. Not only does a fireplace add charm, light, and warmth to the

Opposite A beautifully austere kitchen with fifteenth-century stone slab floors once stood alone as a retreat for monks from the nearby Abbaye de Montmajour; a majestic house was later built around it. *Above* An elegant vegetable sink, called a *gatouille*, was carved from marble-like *pierre de Tavel*, stone from the northern Rhône valley, for a kitchen near Saint-Rémy-de-Provence.

Eighteenth-century pots and utensils collected over many years from flea markets, estate sales, and auctions adorn a vintage *potager,* or hob stove, in an alcove of a Paris kitchen.

kitchen, but it also serves a defined culinary purpose. Fire cooks a roast to perfection, whether it be a plump guinea hen on a rotisserie or a leg of lamb hanging by a string (*à la ficelle*) from a sturdy fireplace hook. Some fireplaces encompass a classic *potager*—a hob stove—next to the hearth for other forms of cooking. The *potager*, which literally translates as "soup-maker," has vaulted niches in the center and cast-iron *plaques*, or "burners," on the top, often faced with glazed tile. Coals from the fire were transferred into the niches and replenished often, which kept the burners on top hot enough to keep pots placed over them simmering. Big pots of stew or soup— *potage* in French, whence the name *potager*— would cook slowly all day, and sometimes all night. The pot-au-feu, composed of a variety of meats with root vegetables and sometimes cabbage, is a classic dish that dates from the days when the fireplace and its *potager* were the only means of cooking.

Among the most distinctive characteristics of the French country kitchens I visited, and featured here in the following pages, is the acknowledgment of the past in some way, either as inspiration or to respect the kitchen's "old bones"—the walls, the beams, the floors, the volumes—or to use old vintage elements, cooking tools, or art, even in a very contemporary kitchen design. One aspect of the French kitchen that intrigues and impresses me particularly is the imaginative use of "found" elements. In a kitchen I saw in Saint-Rémy (pages 123–29), part of a century-old wrought-iron gate covers storage shelves beneath the sink. In another home I visited south of Paris, old window shutters found at a flea market are reborn as cabinet doors. Kitchen closet doors built into walls in at least a score of the kitchens I saw started life two hundred years ago as part of a walnut, oak, or pine armoire. There always seems to be at least one note of *nostalgie,* if not more, in the French country kitchen.

I was surprised to discover that in quite a few of these kitchens, the most modern and technologically advanced accoutrements, such as state-of-the-art dishwashers, freezers, and even refrigerators, were hidden away in an *arrière-cuisine,* a back kitchen. Back kitchens—once pantries, washrooms, or, in old farmhouses, stables—also offer generous storage options for cookware, dry goods, and canned goods. Some of them have second refrigerators and second ovens, practical for large-scale entertaining. Even in cases where there is no second kitchen, owners take care to cover up the refrigerator or dishwasher discreetly, and hide the appliances behind a curtain of checked or printed cotton, or perhaps heavy beige linen.

The strong sense of place evoked by the décor, and by the respect for local style and traditions, is another admirable element of the French country kitchen. Home owners renovating, redecorating, or building a kitchen from the ground up will usually favor local materials—ceramic or cement tiles from the local tile company; wrought-iron window frames, chandeliers, or cabinet facings from the ironmonger in the next town; wicker chairs and storage baskets custom woven for the room; a salvaged stone sink, ceiling

An elegantly detailed eighteenth-century egg cooker still does its job with élan in Philippe Irrmann's Paris kitchen.

Above In a cozy farmhouse kitchen in Brittany, a vintage cast-iron wood stove heats the room while a cement floor painted paprika-red adds visual warmth. *Opposite* Market-fresh ingredients for a berry clafouti (see the recipe on page 105) await assembly in a farmhouse kitchen near Mas Blanc.

beams, and hand-hewn stones from a barn wall in a razed farmhouse in the region. Granted, this is easier to do when you live somewhere that is surrounded by renowned tile makers, great iron ateliers, and the occasional crumbling seventeenth-century farmhouse, as you are in the heart of Provence. Still, the effort of these home owners to incorporate meaningful local elements is inspiring, and the result is added authenticity and character.

Every French country kitchen reflects the spirit of the house, its owners, and the region, but it is also, and perhaps most important, the source of wonderful homemade regional cuisine. Food is the soul of the kitchen, its raison d'être. For almost every one of the kitchens presented here, we also offer a recipe that was prepared in that kitchen and that represents the culinary style, traditions, and tastes of its owner.

There is, for example, a gratin of eggplant, tomatoes, and red onion from an antique farmhouse kitchen near Saint-Rémy; beggar's purses with salmon, crème fraîche, and herbs from a château kitchen in the Luberon; creamy pumpkin soup from a little kitchen overlooking a garden in Paris; and a glazed apple tart from the beamed kitchen of an eighteenth-century home near Étampes, in the Île-de-France. Our featured kitchens offer a distinct aperçu of the intimate life of France, laying bare the components of French style and French taste, both culinary and decorative. It may be one humble, functional room, but the French country kitchen reveals all you need to know about the art and joy of living in France.

A TASTE FOR TRADITION

THERE IS ENORMOUS RESPECT FOR THE PAST in contemporary French architecture and design, and this is especially true in the realm of kitchen design. Memories macro and micro—from the general feeling of a long-ago kitchen, the way the light filled the room, for example, or the sense of space, to little details such as the colors of the tile on a backsplash, or a hand-stitched linen bag that held a day's leftover baguettes—inspire today's design. ⚘ Not only memories fuel a desire for traditional elements and design. The desire can spring from a love of old craftsmanship, and a nostalgia for earlier times. Each of the kitchens presented in this section evokes the past, the beloved traditions of France, in design and ambience. In an eighteenth-century farmhouse kitchen in the Île-de-France, a hilltop aerie in the Vaucluse, a seventeenth-century château in the Luberon, a town house on the River Sorgue, and even in the center of Paris, the past enhances the present in beautiful and distinctive ways. ⚘

A Romantic Country Kitchen in the Île-de-France

THIS PASTORAL PROPERTY just an hour south of Paris could be the setting of a fairy tale. It is imbued with enchantment, and even its name comes from an old European fable, "Puss in Boots." Home to antique dealer Martine Ouvrard, the enclave she's dubbed Le Marquis de Carabas comprises a bucolic eighteenth-century stone farmhouse surrounded by willow trees and gardens, and several outbuildings. One of these is home to her antique shop, which, she explains, offers "only antiques with charm but that aren't too expensive." Everything about the setting, in a village of just fifteen homes surrounded by the flat farmland of the Île-de-France, says "Welcome."

In centuries past, people and animals often lived under the same roof. There was a large common room in the center of the house for the family, with stables flanking each side to provide warmth. Upstairs were the granaries. Chez Martine, the kitchen was once the stable that housed cows and sheep. "I've changed many things here, of course," says Martine. "But I wanted to keep the original stone walls of the room, and the original volume. To enhance the antique ambience, I have always used old, salvaged elements—eighteenth- and nineteenth-century tiles, wood for the beams, and wrought iron for some mullioned windows and

Opposite Original eighteenth-century stone walls married with salvaged elements such as hand-hewn beams and terra-cotta tiles enhance the period ambience of antiques dealer Martine Ouvrard's farmhouse kitchen near Étampes. *Left* Willows shade the rustic stone exterior facing a small garden.

Above, left A winsome hanging bread bag stitched from a vintage monogrammed towel and other period fabrics hangs from a cabinet door near the fireplace. *Above, right* One of Martine's eighteenth-century Provençal quilts covers a Louis XV–style fauteuil near the kitchen's entrance. The pillows are by Linum. *Opposite* Gustavian-style chairs discovered at a flea market and refinished by Martine with a gray patina surround a long French harvest table covered by a contemporary linen quilt with a vintage look. The eighteenth-century-inspired still life painting above the table is by Danielle Mercier.

doors. I created the fireplace, where friends and I often make a fire on cold nights to cook a roast, out of antique bricks and an eighteenth-century cast-iron fireback."

After the essential elements were in place, Martine decorated the room with a combination of French and Swedish Gustavian-style antiques. Gustavian furniture is named for Sweden's eighteenth-century king Gustav V, who brought French style back to Sweden after a visit to Louis XVI's court, and it is very compatible with French antiques. In the harmonious mélange are a long French harvest table, Gustavian-style chairs discovered at a flea market, a three-shelf étagère for displaying soup tureens and silver, and old billiards lamps. The fabrics that brighten the kitchen are a combination of antique tablecloths,

A vintage three-shelf étagère refinished by Martine with a soft, green patina holds a portion of her vast collection of antique porcelain and silver, including soup tureens from Gien in the Loire Valley and Sarreguemines in Lorraine.

antique quilts, and contemporary Swedish textiles. "I find this combination of fabrics very *sympathique*," says Martine.

To keep accent colors in the cream and grayed-down green kitchen soft and to a minimum, Martine chose a refrigerator and a dishwasher sheathed in a satiny silver stainless steel. The kitchen's muted palette even extends to a custom-painted contemporary still life of fruits by French artist Danielle Mercier that dominates one wall in the dining area. What the kitchen initially needed most crucially was natural light. At the front of

To bring light into the once-dark kitchen, Martine pierced a thick stone wall to add a fan-shaped window salvaged from a ruined abbey. A modestly proportioned dishwasher and refrigerator maintain a discreet contemporary presence.

the house, where the kitchen overlooks the garden, Martine installed French doors and mullioned windows in the stone façade. Then came the quest for an interesting old window to install over the sink at the back of the house. She "found her happiness," as the French say, at a salvage house—a demi-lune Palladian-style window from an old abbey. That one element dramatically changed and enhanced the character of the kitchen. "It illuminates the whole kitchen," remarks Martine. "To me, it's like a ray of light from the sun."

Tarte aux Pommes à la Martine
MARTINE'S GLAZED APPLE TART

This simple, classic apple tart has a hint of cinnamon and gets an appealing sheen from its lush apricot glaze. Serve it alone or with a spoonful of crème fraîche. Note that the pastry crust must rest for at least 1 hour before you form the tart. The recipe calls for a touch of kirsch—a cherry brandy—in the glaze, which thins the jam and enhances the fruitiness of the tart.

SERVES 6 TO 8

*For the pâte brisée
(sweetened short-crust pastry)*

1 1/2 cups all-purpose flour

1/2 cup sugar

1/8 teaspoon baking powder

1/4 teaspoon fine sea salt

8 tablespoons (1 stick) unsalted butter, chilled and cut into small pieces

1 large egg, beaten

2 to 3 tablespoons ice water

For the filling

5 Golden Delicious apples, peeled, cored, quartered, and sliced very thin

1/4 cup sugar

1/2 teaspoon ground cinnamon

3 tablespoons unsalted butter, chilled and cut into small pieces

For the apricot glaze

1/2 cup apricot preserves

1 tablespoon kirsch or fresh lemon juice

TO MAKE THE PÂTE BRISÉE: Combine the flour, sugar, baking powder, salt, and butter in a food processor. Process for 10 to 12 seconds, until the mixture has a dry, crumbly texture resembling coarse cornmeal. Add the egg and 2 tablespoons of ice water to the mixture

and pulse 10 to 12 times—just until the dough comes together in a smooth mass, but before it forms a ball.

If the dough seems too dry, add another tablespoon of ice water and pulse for a couple of seconds.

Remove the dough from the bowl and form it into a ball with your hands. If the dough is very sticky, coat your palms with flour once or twice and work it into the dough. (The dough should be malleable and a bit tacky but should not stick to your hands.) Transfer the dough onto a piece of plastic wrap or wax paper, press it into a flat disk, wrap it well, and refrigerate for at least 1 hour.

On a floured work surface, use a floured rolling pin to roll out the chilled dough into a large circle 1/8 inch thick and about 13 inches in diameter. Transfer the pastry circle to a buttered 10 1/2-inch removable-bottom tart pan and gently press the dough into the bottom and fluted sides. Trim the dough so that just 1 inch extends above the rim. Fold the excess dough over on itself to create a double-thick 1/4-inch border. Flute the edges, prick the bottom of the pastry shell with a fork, cover with plastic wrap, and refrigerate for 15 minutes.

TO MAKE THE TART: Preheat the oven to 375°F.

Arrange the apples on the pastry in overlapping concentric circles, starting at the outside edge and working into the center. In a small bowl, combine the sugar and cinnamon and sprinkle over the apples. Dot the top of the tart evenly with the chilled butter pieces. Bake the tart in the center of the oven until the apples are a golden brown, about 35 minutes. Cool on a wire rack until lukewarm, about 30 minutes.

TO MAKE THE APRICOT GLAZE: Melt the preserves in a small saucepan over medium meat, stirring occasionally. Remove from the heat, stir in the kirsch or lemon juice, and strain immediately into a small bowl. When the tart has cooled to lukewarm, apply the warm glaze over the surface of the apples with a pastry brush. If the glaze thickens before you've brushed it on, add a tablespoon of water and reheat. Let the tart rest for at least half an hour before serving.

CHANTEDUC IDYLL:
AT HOME IN PROVENCE
WITH PATRICIA WELLS

FROM THEIR HOME on a hillside high above the medieval city of Vaison-la-Romaine, food writer Patricia Wells and her husband, Walter, enjoy the kind of views Provençal dreams are made of. There is little in the views of vineyard and woodland that gives a clue to what century you are in, so pristine are the surroundings. The rolling green landscape, warmed by the Mediterranean sun, is dotted here and there with a slanted terra-cotta roof . . . but not many. Patricia and Walter found their eighteenth-century *mas*, or farmhouse, several years ago and fell in love with the setting instantly. The property is surrounded by pine trees and oaks, olive trees and grapevines, and the gardens flourish with herbs, capers, and a bounty of vegetables.

The couple spent several years turning it slowly into their dream retreat, with a swimming pool, gardens, and a trellised dining terrace that is cooled by sweet breezes. This is Chanteduc, the Wellses' haven of privacy, far from their urban lives in Paris.

At the heart of the Wells home, not surprisingly, is the kitchen, once the farmhouse's family room. "I wanted the kitchen to look like it had always been there," says Patricia. "A place to cook with friends. And a kitchen that was as true to the place as possible." To this end, she used many elements crafted

Patricia Wells fills the kitchen of her Provençal farmhouse, Chanteduc (*left*), with marvelous flea-market finds, including a collection of hand-carved wooden cutting boards and an unusual screened *garde-manger*, or food storage cabinet (*opposite*), in which she stores her cheeses at room temperature before serving.

by local artisans and detailed the room with antiques and vintage items, such as the charming little nineteenth-century screened *garde-manger,* which she found at local antiques dealers and salvage houses.

Perhaps the most important element in this luminous, pale yellow kitchen is the center island, with storage below and a vast top of mottled yellow glazed tiles surrounding a marble pastry slab, installed both for its practicality and to break up the sea of tile. The same tiles form the backsplash and the countertops by the sink under the window. Custom slat-seated stools that fit snugly under the island were inspired by vintage garden furniture on the deck, and were created by a local furniture maker. "If it doesn't have an island, it's not a kitchen!" Patricia says. "Other essentials for me were a fireplace, for both cooking and ambience, and two sinks—you *definitely* need two sinks! One is a beautiful nineteenth-century marble sink I found at the Chabaud salvage house in Apt, where I found so many other great architectural elements. I also wanted a real bread oven, which we installed outside on the terrace because it gives off so much heat." Patricia cooks on a cherished vintage La Cornue range, a treasure because it once belonged to Julia Child. "For me," says Patricia, "it's akin to a psychiatrist's owning Freud's couch."

Under whitewashed beams, Patricia's Chanteduc kitchen boasts all of her favorite things: a commanding center island with a wooden cutting board and a marble pastry slab, a fireplace, and two sinks. She found her glorious yellow-glazed tiles in Paris at Les Carrelages du Marais.

Above, left Standing in front of her treasured La Cornue range, which once belonged to Julia Child, Patricia prepares a bowl of red bell pepper and tomato sauce to accompany sautéed polenta wedges. *Above, right* A striking nineteenth-century double sink hand-carved from local granite makes the center island visually dramatic as well as practical. *Opposite, left* A local carpenter created Patricia's slat-seated kitchen stools, inspired by vintage garden furniture. *Opposite, right* A double-framed antique commercial clock keeps track of the time above two vintage cutting boards resting on the terra-cotta-tiled countertop.

Patricia's harmoniously laid out kitchen, with a bird's-eye view of the woodland below from a small window facing west, is the welcoming setting for her renowned cooking course, At Home with Patricia Wells: Cooking in Provence, which books up more than a year in advance. Here, small groups of ten mince, chop, and sauté alongside Patricia, dine at the region's finest bistros and restaurants, and scour the markets for the day's best products.

Some weeks have special themes. Fish Week in Provence, for example, offers visits

to the great fish markets of Marseille, a trip out on a fishing boat into the waters of the Mediterranean, dinners in fish bistros, and several fish prep classes at home with Patricia, preparing the meals and dining at Chanteduc. Students learn how to work with all kinds of fish and shellfish, using the techniques of smoking, braising, grilling, deep-frying, or cooking in parchment. One of the classes includes a presentation by a professional fishmonger, who instructs students on how to fillet a variety of fish, and how to easily open shellfish.

And then there's Truffle Week, an homage to the ultimate French ingredient, featuring black truffle workshops, a black truffle hunt in the woods, black truffle and wine tastings, and of course black truffle dinners. The truffle dinners, as well as other feasts prepared by or with Patricia Wells, are a unique experience for the gastronome, in a memorable and very personal setting. The heart of Chanteduc is the luminous food lovers' kitchen, perfectly adapted to preparing meals for a crowd, or for just one happy couple.

Polenta Poêlée aux Poivrons Rouges et aux Tomates Pimentées

POLENTA WEDGES WITH SPICY RED BELL PEPPER AND TOMATO SAUCE

When I visited Chanteduc, the enchanted private domain of Patricia Wells and her husband, Walter, Patricia prepared a delightful lunch on her trellised terrace. On the menu were these delicious polenta wedges accompanied by a spicy red bell pepper and tomato sauce with onions, cumin, and ground Espelette pepper, a potent red chili pepper from the Basque region. "I love the soothing satisfaction one derives from the creamy flavor, smooth texture, and golden hue of a well-made polenta," says Patricia. With the polenta wedges, Patricia served a bright, dry Sauvignon Blanc.

SERVES 8

For the spicy red bell pepper and tomato sauce

2 tablespoons cumin seeds

4 red bell peppers (about 1½ pounds)

2 tablespoons extra-virgin olive oil

1 teaspoon fine sea salt

2 medium onions, halved and thinly sliced

1 teaspoon ground *piment d'Espelette*
or ground cayenne red pepper

2 pounds ripe, red tomatoes, cored and cubed

For the polenta wedges

3 cups nonfat milk

1 teaspoon fine sea salt

½ teaspoon freshly grated nutmeg

1 cup instant polenta (yellow cornmeal)

1 cup freshly grated Parmigiano-Reggiano cheese

1 tablespoon extra-virgin olive oil

TO MAKE THE SAUCE: Place the cumin seeds in a small nonstick frying pan over moderate heat. Shake the pan regularly until the grains of cumin become fragrant and evenly toasted, about 2 minutes. (They can burn quickly, so watch carefully!) Transfer the cumin to a large plate to cool and set aside.

Quarter the peppers lengthwise and remove and discard all seeds and membranes. Cut each quarter lengthwise into ⅛-inch strips. Set aside.

In a large, heavy-duty casserole, combine the olive oil, salt, onions, *piment d'Espelette,* and heated cumin seeds, stirring to coat the ingredients well with the oil. Cook the mixture slowly over low heat with the lid on, stirring occasionally, until soft, 3 to 4 minutes. Add the bell pepper strips and the tomatoes, cover, and cook over low heat, stirring occasionally, until the peppers are soft and meltingly tender, about 30 minutes.

TO MAKE THE POLENTA: Meanwhile, in a large, heavy-duty saucepan, bring the milk, salt, and nutmeg to a boil over high heat. Watch the pan carefully, as the milk will boil over quickly. Add the dry polenta in a steady stream, stirring constantly with a wooden spoon. Cook until thickened and the polenta easily releases from the side of the pan as it is stirred, about 2 minutes. Remove from the heat, stir in the cheese, and blend thoroughly.

Pour into a 10½-inch round pie dish. Even out the top with a spatula and let cool until firm, about 5 minutes.

Cut the polenta into 8 even wedges. Heat the olive oil over medium-high heat in a large, nonstick skillet, brushing the oil over the bottom of the pan with a pastry brush. Add the polenta slices and cook until browned on both sides, about 1 minute per side. To serve, place a polenta wedge on each plate and top with a generous spoonful or two of the spicy red bell pepper and tomato sauce.

A Château Kitchen
Returns to Its Roots

When your kitchen opens directly onto your opulent château living room, considering the sight lines from the upholstered fauteuils to the massive La Cornue range is of paramount importance. "The kitchen had to have elegant lines and luxurious details to create a natural flow between the rooms," observes French decorator Aline Steinbach, remembering the decorative mandates of her Luberon property, the Château de Céris. Aline—former owner of the fashionable interior design shop Camille en Provence, in Lumières—and her antiques specialist husband, Erwin, bought the property in the mid-1990s, and over several years totally restored and decorated it.

The Château de Céris, which dates from 1680, sits on a hill overlooking the rus-

tic Provençal countryside of Luoux. It was originally constructed as a summerhouse for the Marquis de Chausse-Grosse—Marquis Big Boots!—who resided in Aix-en-Provence. It was cooler here in the Luberon, high on a hill, than in sun-baked Aix. The little village of Luoux is famous in local lore as a stopping point for the legendary military commander Hannibal, who passed through in 218 B.C. on his great march from Spain, over the Alps and into Italy, with massive armies and thirty-seven war elephants. (The town's ancient crest actually features an elephant.)

Opposite Double doors open from the Burgundy-hued living room into a gracious kitchen crowned with a sparkling Napoleon III chandelier at Aline and Erwin Steinbach's Château de Céris in Luoux. *Left* Erwin stops by the château for lunch with Walling, his Dutch Frisian steed.

Aline replaced a small, mundane fireplace with an imposing La Cornue cooktop and surrounded it with a seventeenth-century-style mantel, creating a new kitchen "hearth." She added copper molds to reflect glints of light from the back of the stovetop alcove. For the Louis XVI–style chairs surrounding the nineteenth-century trompe l'oeil painted table Aline chose a 1950s striped Italian jacquard fabric.

Part of the château, particularly the kitchen, was demolished in an ill-conceived restoration in the 1950s and '60s. Many classical architectural elements were removed and sold off to antique dealers and salvage houses. "When we bought the house," says Aline, "the kitchen was a disaster. There was a small, ugly, stupid little fireplace. I wanted to replace it with the big and beautiful La Cornue, stretch out granite counters on either side of it, then create a large beautiful mantel to frame it. The La Cornue—the largest they make, with seven burners—

became our hearth. I did a lot of research on historic fireplaces, and at last found exactly what I wanted in old documents of a seventeenth-century fireplace in a château in the south of France. Château kitchens traditionally had huge fireplaces."

Beneath the vast stovetop, called an *entablement* in French, Aline designed and installed long, deep drawers to keep her cookware out of sight but within easy reach. Matching drawers under the large sink hide kitchen products and tools, and one large sliding drawer hides the garbage can. The

The surfaces of the center island, the countertops, and the backsplash are a testament to Aline's passion for red Italian granite, and her long quest to find just the right slabs with distinctive black veins. Custom cabinetry designed by Aline was finished in place with a deep mahogany-like patina. Small cabochons of red marble dot the Italian porcelain tile floors.

Above An unusually shallow sink in red Italian granite to match the countertops sits to the right of the cooktop for rinsing fruit or vegetables while cooking. *Opposite* A nineteenth-century *buffet à deux corps* displays Aline's collection of antique stemware, always stored stem up to keep the glasses dust free.

oven has been relegated to the *arrière-cuisine,* or back kitchen. There are two ovens in the back, in fact—one on top of the other. "I don't like to bend down to an oven," says Aline. "I hate the heat on my legs. So I installed two wall ovens, one on top of the other." The back kitchen also harbors a washer-dryer, a freezer, a second stove, and two refrigerators. The centerpiece of the back kitchen is a *meuble de métier,* a reproduction of a grain drawer, bought new and finished with an antique patina. The vibrant painting over the buffet, *Nature morte au kilim,* is by the late Gérard Bressan, a Provençal painter who lived in a house nearby.

With the La Cornue established as the long-view focal point, Aline then set about searching for a distinctive chandelier, one that would catch the eye from afar. She sought a fixture with colored bobeches, prisms, and pendants to add sparkle to the room. The quest to find one at markets and auctions in Paris and Provence was disappointing until one day at a flea market she spotted *"la carcasse,"* the skeleton of a handsome Napoleon III chandelier in semi-ruin, with most of its crystals missing. "It was perfect, in spite of its condition," she recalls.

Aline scoured other flea markets and eventually found crystal pendants in the clear and coppery tones she had envisioned. Later on she added a set of gleaming copperware molds over the stove to pick up the color and sparkle of the rust-colored crystal pendants. "I needed something sumptuous over the table," she notes, "since the door opens onto the living room, and the kitchen is on view

when there are guests sitting in the living room. I needed a thread to carry the theme of elegance and opulence from the living room to the kitchen. The chandelier provides the perfect link."

Fleshing out the kitchen design are handsome cabinets built in Avignon that were installed unpainted, then finished in place. Aline wanted to supervise the work in the actual light of her kitchen; the result is a mahogany-like patina, a distinctive deep red with subtle veins of black running through it. The countertops are red granite from Italy. "I chose it," says Aline, "for its beautiful vein. I was looking for a red granite with a black vein, and I looked at many huge slabs until I found the one I loved." In addition to the granite countertops for food preparation, Aline also needed a center island. "I love it for preparing the plates just before serving, or for setting out food for an informal dinner." In the center is a large La Cornue butcher block, flanked on each side by slabs of red granite. The floors are made of large Italian porcelain ceramic tiles resembling travertine, dotted with small cabochons of red marble that repeat the color of the red granite countertops.

The kitchen boasts two sinks: one deep, for washing dishes, and one barely an inch deep, called a *gatouille,* for rinsing vegetables and silverware. The *gatouille* is traditionally positioned right next to the stove. "For the little vegetable sink, I wanted red granite to match the countertops," says Aline, "but for the other sink, much larger and deeper, I chose an American stainless-

steel Breuer. I wanted something very practical and more forgiving than stone for this sink—a glass or a plate might have a chance if you dropped it."

Completing Aline's kitchen mise-en-scène are both vintage and reproduction furniture. Under the dazzling chandelier, a long, large nineteenth-century trompe l'oeil library table from the Berry region of France commands the center of the kitchen, surrounded by 1950s reproductions of Louis XVI fauteuils, reupholstered by Aline in vintage Italian striped jacquard fabric. Aline restored the chairs in her workshop, where she creates furniture, curtains, and accessories for some of the Luberon's most exclusive properties. To the left of the La Cornue "hearth," an imposing *buffet à deux corps,* or chest-on-chest, holds Aline's twinkling collection of vintage stemware.

"For me, the kitchen is the most important room of the house," says Aline, surveying her domain. "It's where family always gathers and friends sit when I'm preparing dinner. I wanted the room to have a feeling of space, luxury, and warmth. It's my refuge when I come home from work, where I love to have a glass of wine. And it's close to the salon, too, so with the door open, I don't feel too isolated when my guests are there having an aperitif before dinner."

Opposite The focal point of the back kitchen is a vibrantly hued painting, *Nature morte au kilim,* by Provençal painter Gérard Bressan, which hangs above a vintage-style reproduction grain cabinet that Aline finished with an antique patina. She filled the glass panels of the drawers with the grains they might once have held.

Aumonières au Saumon

BEGGAR'S PURSES WITH SALMON, CRÈME FRAÎCHE, AND HERBS

❧

These "beggar's purses" are elegant and impressive, yet very easy to make. Each purse is a generous single serving, perfect for a lovely light lunch or a sumptuous first course at dinner. You can do the prep work ahead of time, refrigerating the purses for a few hours and then cooking them just before serving. You can also prepare this dish with fresh tuna or orange roughy instead of salmon. When using phyllo pastry, be sure to keep all but the phyllo sheets you are working with covered with a slightly damp paper towel; phyllo dough begins to dry out with the merest whisper of air. Aline serves the salmon with an arugula, cherry tomato, and Parmesan salad and roasted asparagus—asparagus drizzled with a bit of extra-virgin olive oil and aged balsamic vinegar, then baked in a 400°F. oven until browned, about 6 minutes.

SERVES 6

1½ pounds center-cut salmon fillet, cut into 1-inch cubes

½ cup crème fraîche

½ cup chopped fresh dill, or 2 tablespoons dried

½ cup chopped fresh mint or basil

½ teaspoon fine sea salt

Freshly ground black pepper

18 (17 x 13-inch) sheets frozen phyllo dough, thawed

6 tablespoons unsalted butter, melted

1 small bunch chives, optional

Preheat the oven to 400°F.

In a medium bowl, combine the salmon, crème fraîche, dill, mint, salt, and several twists of pepper; stir gently with a wooden spoon to combine. Set aside.

Unfold the phyllo sheets on a baking pan or other flat surface; cover with a barely damp paper or linen towel to prevent them from drying out and becoming brittle. For each beggar's purse, you will need three sheets of phyllo dough. Cover your work surface with a sheet of parchment paper. Cover a baking sheet with another sheet of parchment paper and set aside. Remove one sheet of phyllo dough and place it on the work surface. Brush with the melted butter. Layer on another sheet of phyllo and brush with butter. Layer on the third sheet of phyllo and brush with butter. Spoon one sixth of the salmon mixture onto the center of the sheet. Gather the phyllo into a snug "purse" and pinch the neck together, twisting slightly at the same time. Wrap the neck a couple of times around with kitchen twine to secure and tie in a bow. Place on the prepared baking sheet and set aside. Repeat with the remaining phyllo sheets and salmon mixture, forming six large beggar's purses. (At this point, you can store the purses in the refrigerator for up to 4 hours, covered lightly with plastic wrap. Remove from the refrigerator 20 minutes before baking; remove the plastic wrap.) Bake the purses in the center of the oven for about 10 minutes, until the gathered edges of each purse turn golden brown. For a decorative touch, slip one or two long, graceful chives into the neck of each purse just before serving. Serve immediately.

Michel Biehn's Nostalgic "Grandmother's Kitchen"

Michel Biehn, a renowned expert and dealer in vintage Provençal textiles, lives and works in a handsome nineteenth-century home built by a prosperous wool merchant. It is located in the town of L'Isle-sur-la-Sorgue, the largest enclave of antiques dealers anywhere in France outside of Paris. While the living quarters are upstairs, the traditional Provençal kitchen is downstairs, just off the broad foyer leading to the rooms of Michel's alluring shop. Today the kitchen looks just like a classic "grandmother's kitchen," unchanged over the generations, but it wasn't always so.

"When we bought the house in the early 1990s, the kitchen had been 'modernized,'" relates Michel, "transformed into someone's vision of a dream 1970s kitchen with violently colored tilework from the period, modern appliances, and old architectural details, such as the original fireplace, plastered over. A few elements survived the 1970s renovation, including a large wooden cupboard and the marble sink. We set to work to return the kitchen to how it might have originally looked a hundred years ago."

One of the first orders of business was putting in a fireplace. Michel knew there had been one originally, because the chimney leading down to it could be seen on the roof. He was delighted to discover

Opposite Vibrant blue-and-white Provençal tiles salvaged from a nineteenth-century house in Carpentras highlight the lovingly re-created "grandmother's kitchen" of Michel Biehn's ivy-covered home in L'Isle-sur-la-Sorgue (*left*).

that the brick fireplace had remained intact inside the wall, as had the flue and chimney. He designed a mantelpiece based on traditional nineteenth-century regional styles to surround it, and had it made in plaster by a local artisan. The glowing nineteenth-century blue-and-white tiles around the stove and the fireplace were salvaged from an old home in the nearby town of Carpentras, one built at about the same time as Michel's. Next came the search for a stove that was modern and functional but with a nineteenth-century *esprit.* Michel chose a brass-trimmed, black French Lacanche range with both gas and electric burners. For the flooring, he installed handsome and resilient black marble terrazzo slabs, a composition of pressed and polished marble chips. Appliances that ease twenty-first-century life, such as the dishwasher and the large refrigerator and freezer, have been relegated to a back room, out of sight but within easy reach.

When it came to furnishing the room, Michel had specific ideas about what he wanted in the way of a dining table, storage, and decoration. The rectangular table in the middle of the room, designed by Michel with a lava stone top and a wrought-iron base

Michel's recast old-fashioned kitchen is all about unpretentious comfort and authenticity. After he discovered a concealed fireplace, he designed the nineteenth-century-style Provençal mantelpiece to surround it. Today it's a convenient resting place for the whimsical faience dog by Provençal ceramist and painter Gérard Drouillet. Next he added a brass-trimmed Lacanche range with nineteenth-century *esprit.* In the center of the black marble terrazzo slab floor, custom-designed wicker chairs surround a lava-stone and wrought-iron table.

Previous pages, left A trough-shaped marble sink is one of the few remaining elements from the original nineteenth-century kitchen. Below the sink are three baskets designed by the same artisan who created the dining chairs. *Previous pages, right* Michel added vintage brass faucets and a rustic *vaisselier* shelf for drying large bowls, pots, and pitchers. *Above* A large wooden cabinet from the 1930s survived an ill-conceived 1970s renovation. *Opposite, left* In front of the fireplace, a vintage mosaic pot created from broken bits of crockery holds a bouquet of utensils. *Opposite, right* Above the stove, a wrought-iron pot rack offers practical storage for pots, lids, and ladles.

forged by a local *ferronnier*, or iron craftsman, works both for dining and for food preparation. "This kitchen has no counter space, as was the case with most old kitchens, so I needed a table that could function as an island as well." In counterpoint to the substantial table, the chairs of woven wicker are light and graceful. "For me," says Michel, "a table must be heavy and stable, but the chairs must be light, and easy to move. I hate heavy chairs!"

"I was having a local basket maker create some market-style baskets to slide under the kitchen sink to store cleaning products and refuse," Michel continues, "so I thought I'd ask him if he could execute a set of chairs that I had designed. He did them perfectly. I think the three baskets are a nice echo of the chairs. You don't want to have too many different textures and materials in a kitchen."

A variety of eclectic *objets*, such as the vintage blue-and-white pitchers from Normandy, Morocco, and Provence; a large, whimsical faience dog by the artist Gérard Drouillet; ceramic pots; and old copperware cover what little counter space the kitchen offers. Most were picked up in strolls through neighboring antiques dealers in L'Isle-sur-la-Sorgue. "It's not a practical kitchen," Michel admits, "but it's peaceful and harmonious, and I love it."

Poivrons Farcis à la Provençal
PROVENÇAL STUFFED BELL PEPPERS

The texture and flavors in this classic Provençal dish are fabulous! In the filling, along with sunflower seeds, rice, raisins, corn, and pine nuts, Michel (*opposite*) uses tiny green lentils from Le Puy, in the Auvergne region. These are the world's best lentils, often called "caviar du Puy," with a better flavor and texture than the larger and more common brown lentils. Michel serves his savory, colorful peppers as an accompaniment to grilled chicken or pork, or, for a lighter meal, as a main course paired with a mixed-greens salad.

SERVES 6

3 tablespoons extra-virgin olive oil

1 medium onion, finely chopped

1 clove garlic, minced

1 small carrot, peeled and minced

1 cup long-grain rice

½ cup dried tiny green lentils

½ cup fresh corn kernels, or frozen and thawed

⅓ cup raisins

⅓ cup sunflower seeds

⅓ cup pine nuts

½ teaspoon fine sea salt

Freshly ground black pepper

½ cup chopped fresh parsley

½ teaspoon ground *piment d'Espelette* or ground cayenne red pepper

6 large orange, red, or yellow bell peppers

Juice of two lemons

In a medium enamel casserole or a large skillet with a cover, heat the olive oil over medium heat. Add the onion, garlic, and carrot and sauté, stirring frequently, until the onions are soft and translucent but not browned, about 4 minutes. Add the rice, lentils, corn, raisins, sunflower seeds, pine nuts, salt, and several twists of the pepper, and stir to combine. Add enough water to cover the mixture by half an inch, bring to a boil, then reduce the heat, cover, and simmer until the liquid is just absorbed, 10 to 15 minutes. Remove from the heat, and stir in the parsley and *piment d'Espelette*. Adjust the seasonings if necessary and set aside, uncovered.

Preheat the oven to 375°F.

Using a sharp knife, slice off the cap from each pepper half an inch from the top. Reserve the caps. Seed and core the peppers. Slice just enough off the bottom of each pepper to ensure that the peppers stand upright, taking care not to slice into the center of the pepper. Generously but loosely fill each pepper with the rice mixture, then mound the filling above the top of the peppers. Place the peppers in a greased baking dish just large enough to hold them. In a bowl or a measuring cup, combine the lemon juice with 1 cup of water and pour into the baking dish around (but not on) the peppers. Top the peppers with their reserved caps, and bake in the center of the oven for about 40 minutes, until the peppers are softened and beginning to wrinkle and their caps have browned. Serve immediately.

PAST PERFECT: A NEW PARIS KITCHEN MADE OLD

I NSPIRED BY A TIME when the world cooked only by fire, the owner of this remarkable kitchen is a collector with a passion for eighteenth-century furniture and art. It had long been a dream of his to create a kitchen that was true to that time, with every element of the design and every decoration, utensil, and towel originating in the 1700s. Several years ago, when he bought his apartment in the heart of Paris's garment district, he decided to make his dream come true. The kitchen is so authentic to the period, so well executed, that it is hard to believe it is actually less than ten years old, a room created from whole cloth, so to speak. It is as perfect as a movie set.

"Everything in the kitchen is eighteenth-century or older, as it would have been during the 1700s," say the owner. "My wife and I have scouted the Saint-Ouen and Vanves flea markets in Paris, as well as dealers, *brocante* shops, and attic sales over the years, always searching for the perfect elements. All the copper and bronze pots are vintage, as are the terra-cotta *tomettes* [hexagonal tiles]. We even found an intricate eighteenth-century wall clock, one with a timer that was created exclusively for kitchens. Ours was a very specialized quest because, in addition to the items being authentic to the period, they all had to be French."

Opposite Gleaming collections of seventeenth- and eighteenth-century copperware and cooking utensils adorn the walls of Philippe Irrmann's unique period Paris kitchen, where everything—even baked apples, poised on a special eighteenth-century rack just for that purpose (*left*)—is cooked by fire.

A single window overlooking the mottled rooftops of central Paris floods the little kitchen with light during the day, while candlelight and oil lamps—and of course the fireplace—illuminate the room at night. The off-white walls are not painted, explains the owner, but rather are covered with *chaux*—a naturally whitish beige limestone wash—which would have been used in the 1700s. Over the years, smoke and heat from the fire has tinged the fireplace's border brown in spots. Open shelving and pot hooks display most of the cookware, while a small armoire and a low cabinet hold dishes, glassware, linens, and cutlery. Water comes from behind the scenes, from a pantry that has been made into a small, modern kitchen with such basic amenities as a refrigerator, a sink, a stove, and additional storage. This modern little kitchen is for everyday life—morning coffee, a light lunch, or a simple dinner.

The eighteenth-century kitchen is reserved for special occasions. Once a week or so, the owners entertain their friends, giving dinner parties using eighteenth-century recipes and eighteenth-century cooking methods. Dishes are braised, grilled, steamed, boiled, stewed, or baked, with heat coming from the fire below, from hot coals beneath the pot or

The eighteenth-century fireplace, looking as though it has always existed in this spot, is the centerpiece of Philippe's kitchen. Every element is authentic to the period, from the precise arch of the niche below the fireplace to the octagonal tile floors, the woven blue fabrics on the seat cushions, the cutting boards—even the faded strip of blue-and-white fabric that stretches across the fireplace to curtain the smoke.

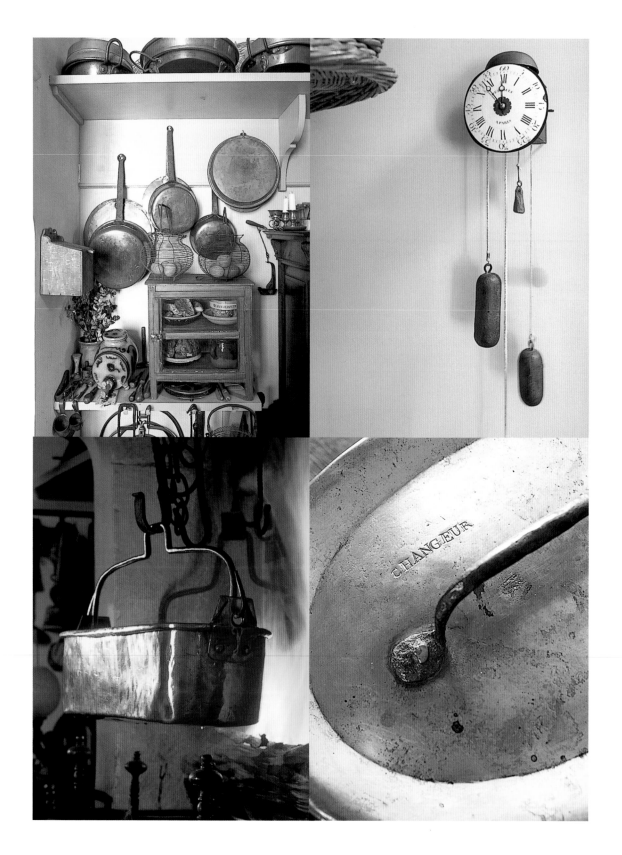

mounded on top of it. Among the house specialties is a succulent pot-au-feu, literally "pot on the fire," a traditional French boiled dinner made from beef or other rich meats combined with root vegetables and cooked in a cast-iron pot suspended over the flames. Other fire-cooked dishes include grilled lobsters with pineapple, stuffed cabbage, roast chicken, jams, baked apples, and assorted fruit clafoutis.

In *À la Recherche du temps perdu*, Marcel Proust set out to capture a lost moment in time from his late-nineteenth-century childhood. Here, surrounded by Paris boulevards teeming with traffic, one couple sought to recreate a different, earlier moment in time, and succeeded memorably.

Opposite, clockwise from above left In an alcove at the kitchen's entrance, a small screen-doored *garde-manger* contains cheeses, nuts, and dried fruits, while a pair of eighteenth-century wire baskets protects fresh eggs; an eighteenth-century wall clock that also functions as a timer works as perfectly today as it did in 1785; during centuries past, when few people had their own large ovens, it was the custom to take large pots to the local baker to have stews or roasts baked in the *boulangerie*'s oven—to prevent loss, owners often stamped their pots with their names, as did the Changeur family; flames accent the handsome hand-hammered surface and gracefully curved wrought-iron handle of a large eighteenth-century copper pot. *Above* An attractive riveted spout and a daintily domed lid distinguish an unusual long-handled eighteenth-century sauce pot.

Pot-au-Feu

BOILED FILET OF BEEF
WITH ROOT VEGETABLES

This French boiled dinner is one of the oldest recipes in the French culinary canon, dating back hundreds of years. It was originally cooked in a big iron pot hung over or next to a fire, or placed over hot coals, and it used an inexpensive piece of beef, sometimes with a marrow bone thrown in for flavor. This recipe, using a rolled filet of beef, is a more luxurious and shorter version of the classic, ready in about two hours. In some homes the pot-au-feu was left to simmer on the stove throughout the day, with whatever bits or pieces of meat or vegetables were left over added along the way. A friend jokes that her grandmother's pot-au-feu had been on the stove for twenty-five years. Serve this dish with boiled potatoes, cooked separately, and strong Dijon mustard. Strain the broth and reserve to use as bouillon or stock in other recipes (or as the base for another pot-au-feu!). The leftover boiled lamb and veal can be used, ground up or minced, for a delicious shepherd's pie, a dish the French call *hachis Parmentier*.

SERVES 6 TO 8

5 tablespoons olive oil

3 small onions, peeled (one of them quartered)

$^1/_2$ pound pancetta, coarsely chopped

1 pound lamb shoulder

1 pound veal knuckle

1 teaspoon sugar

Fine sea salt

2 pounds carrots, peeled and cut into 2-inch pieces

2 medium leeks, white and pale green parts only, carefully washed and cut into 2-inch pieces

1 Savoy cabbage, quartered

3 small turnips, peeled and quartered

3 leafy stalks fennel

5 whole garlic cloves, peeled

1 orange, cut into 4 large slices

Zest of one lemon

1 bouquet garni consisting of 1 sprig each parsley, tarragon, and cilantro and $^1/_2$ cinnamon stick tied in a cheesecloth sack

8 black peppercorns

4 whole cloves

$3^1/_2$- to 4-pound rolled and tied filet of beef prepared by your butcher (leave two long ends of butcher's string attached to each end of the filet)

In a large, heavy-bottomed casserole or a soup pot, heat 3 tablespoons of the olive oil over medium-high heat. Add the quartered onion, pancetta, lamb, and veal and brown on all sides, stirring frequently, until the meats begin to release their juices, about 10 minutes. Add the sugar and a generous pinch of salt and stir to combine. Do not let the onion turn brown; if it starts taking on too much color, scrape it to the side of the pot, or remove it until the meats are browned. Add the carrots, leeks, cabbage, turnips, fennel, garlic, orange, lemon zest, bouquet garni, and peppercorns. Stick 2 of the cloves into each of the two remaining whole onions and add to the pot. Fill the pot three-quarters full with cold water, and bring the mixture to a boil over high heat. Skim off any froth that rises to the surface. Reduce the heat to medium, cover, and cook for 1 hour, stirring and skimming occasionally. Remove from the heat and set aside for 20 to 30 minutes.

Meanwhile, use the lengths of string at each end of the beef filet to suspend it from the handle of a wooden spoon large enough to sit across the top of the pot. The beef should cook in the middle of the pot surrounded by the bouillon, but not touching the bottom of the pot, where it could cook unevenly. (If you don't have a long wooden spoon, hang the beef from a long metal skewer or skimming spoon.)

Lower the filet of beef into the pot, making sure that it is covered by bouillon on all sides. Bring the broth to a full, rolling boil. Lower the heat to medium-high and cook at a low boil for 30 minutes. Check the seasonings, adding more salt to taste. Remove from the heat and transfer the beef filet to a platter. Pat dry with paper towels.

In a skillet, heat the remaining 2 tablespoons of olive oil over high heat, then add the beef filet and quickly brown it on all sides, 4 to 5 minutes. You just want to color the filet, not cook it further. Slice the beef and arrange on a warmed platter surrounded by the vegetables. Serve with boiled potatoes and hot mustard and/or horseradish sauce.

TILE WORKS

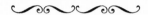

A COUNTRY ENDOWED WITH A TOPOGRAPHY THAT CONTAINS LARGE DEPOSITS OF QUALITY CLAY, FRANCE HAS A WEALTH OF CERAMICS CENTERS THAT DATE BACK CENTURIES. THESE CENTERS SPRUNG UP AND THRIVED BECAUSE IN ADDITION TO LOCAL CLAY, THEY WERE near forests that provided wood to fire the kiln, and natural springs that provided water to moisten and mix with the clay. More than a score of renowned faience and pottery towns now produce a vast array of clay creations, from tiny figurines to enormous pots large enough to hold an orange tree. These include Desvres in the north of France; Gien in the Loire region; Quimper in Brittany; Anduze and Uzès in the Gard; Salernes, Moustiers, Aubagne, and Apt in Provence; and Biot and Vallauris on the Riviera. Beautiful tiles of every variety—large, small, glazed, unglazed, of white clay, of red clay, of mixed clays, flat, embossed, simple, or ornate—are among the most prized and sought-after products of these ceramics centers, and their primary destination is French country kitchens.

Very few French kitchens have no tile at all. Tiles create an extremely practical and generally durable surface for countertops, backsplashes, fireplace trim, tabletops, and of course flooring. Tile work can be subtle and subdued—white or cream with discreet-contrast trim in gray or beige, for example—or it can be bold and graphic, featuring large squares in red and yellow, or a vibrant multicolored patchwork. The effect can be monochromatic, with the countertop and backsplash tiled in a single, large-scaled tile, or can represent a full palette of colors.

Most tile work is created from solid-colored tiles, which achieve depth and variation through the hand-glazing process, giving each tile its own color gradations and character. A monochromatic surface is not necessarily flat, atonal, or uninteresting. When the tiles are decorated, the pattern is usually geometric, or a tiny Delft-like design—a cobalt blue leaf or blossom, or an elegant squiggle in the corner of a white tile. What you do not see in the best kitchens is tile work depicting the clichéd images of "country French" style—lemons, roosters, or garlands of flowers.

Ceramic flooring tiles are most often produced in some form of terra-cotta, perhaps in a square tile, or perhaps in the vintage-looking hexagonal tiles called *tomettes,* a legacy of the eighteenth century. One of the most important centers today for French terra-cotta tiles is the Provençal town of Salernes, in the Var. Terra-cotta tiles from Salernes and elsewhere in France are available in a wide variety of pink, orange, red, and yellow natural clay hues—from palest peach to deep brick red. A soft pink shade with a timeworn look is one of the most popular and versatile colors. All terra-cotta gives off a warm glow, keeps a room

A vibrant sample board at the Vernin Carreaux D'Apt tile works in Bonnieux displays a composition of more than seven different colors. The combination has been one of the company's best-sellers for more than twenty years.

Clockwise from above left Intricate mosaic patterned tiles border a fireplace in the Luberon; diagonally set red and yellow tiles form the backsplash for an outdoor faucet in the Alpilles; hand-painted blue-and-white nineteenth-century Provençal tiles in a variety of patterns border a fireplace in the Vaucluse; boldly patterned cement tiles combine to form a geometric backsplash in a rustic kitchen near Dijon; a checkerboard of early-twentieth-century cement tiles from Provence welcomes visitors to the Clos des Saumanes, a bed-and-breakfast near Avignon; a graphically striped border of contemporary cement tiles brightens a kitchen in Saint-Laurent-d'Aigouze.

cool in the summer, retains heat in the winter, and is easy to maintain and keep clean.

Beyond terra-cotta, some of the most distinctive and interesting-looking floors I've come across are created from vintage-looking cement tiles, replicas of tiles that represented the height of fashion in France, Belgium, and England from the 1890s to about 1920. Thicker than clay tiles and extremely durable, with a smooth, satiny surface, cement tiles are produced by a very different method from traditional clay tiles. They are created by pouring a variety of colored mortars into patterned sections of a stencil-like brass or bronze mold, then steam-pressed to fix the colors of the newly formed tile. (The technical term is "encaustic tiles," a nineteenth-century phrase connoting tiles in which the surface pattern comes not from a glaze but from a precise mix of different-colored clays.) The tiles are then left to dry for several weeks in temperature- and humidity-controlled drying rooms instead of being fired in a kiln, so that heat does not alter their color or form.

Clockwise from above left Vintage blue-and-white Desvres tiles once made in northern France enliven the countertop, backsplash, and windowsill of a seventeenth-century country house in the Île-de-France; floral-patterned tiles bordering the range hood enhance the garden theme set by the custom trellis design of the backsplash, composed of flat white tiles separated by slim green raised tile strips; glazed ocher and Bordeaux handmade tiles from Vernin Carreaux D'Apt form a vibrant backsplash in an apartment kitchen in Avignon (the place mat is from Les Olivades); early twentieth-century tiles from an old patisserie were salvaged to adorn a restored farmhouse kitchen; reflecting the colors of the Provençal landscape, mottled terra-cotta tiles bordered in olive green add warmth to the countertop, backsplash, and center island of a small kitchen in the Bouches-du-Rhone.

Cement tiles, sometimes still called encaustic tiles, are once again fashionable yet still "old-fashioned." The designs and colors of new cement tiles reflect the turn-of-the-nineteenth-century heyday of the originals: graceful Belle Époque geometric patterns, often with an Art Nouveau look, as well as neo-Gothic motifs that were popular in Victorian England. Predominant colors are subdued tones of blue, tan, gray, charcoal, mustard, and russet. Vintage cement tiles—and entire floors salvaged from old houses—are very sought after by architects and designers (see Source Guide, page 216, for dealers). New cement tiles are made by a number of venerable firms, including Carocim in Puyricard, near Aix-en-Provence, and Josse, in Plancoët, on the northern coast of Brittany.

One of my happiest visual memories of the

French countryside is of a run-down (and cheap!) villa I rented years ago in the Var region of Provence, with a terrace that overlooked unkempt gardens full of lemon and almond trees. The interior, while simply furnished, boasted some of the most striking floors I had ever seen. The house was built in 1910 and the flooring—vintage cement tiles produced in Aix-en-Provence in lavish patterns and restrained colors—dated from that year. Each room had a different floor, which was nevertheless compatible and harmonious with the floors that abutted it. The floors comprised a fantastic mélange of designs—frieze work, arabesque patterns, Greek key motifs, trompe l'oeil cubes, and harlequin squares. I've rarely seen a house like this since, and always wondered what became of it. It was a living museum of early-twentieth-century floor design in France.

STYLISH SIMPLICITY

IN KITCHEN DESIGN, AMONG THE MOST prized attributes is excellent organization—the lack of clutter, an airy and practical work environment, and easy storage—using high-quality basic materials such as marble, wood, tile, and stone. The four kitchens featured here—in a village home in the Alpilles, in a cottage surrounded by olive groves, in a nineteenth-century apartment in Paris, and in a farmhouse near Saint-Rémy-de-Provence—encompass all of these desirable traits. Each highlights the simplicity and straightforwardness of design that was each owner's mandate. The pristine surfaces, the thoughtfully organized storage, the general lack of "stuff" everywhere, and, above all, the personal resolve and restraint required to maintain such an environment is inspiring indeed! ❧

Practical and Pristine: The Uncluttered Kitchen

PROTECTED BY STONE WALLS and tall iron gates at the edge of a village in the Alpilles is a beautifully restored seventeenth-century home. Its pristine kitchen, extensively renovated, opens onto a terrace that leads into lush gardens and a pool—a little paradise. Over the course of two centuries the original small house was joined by one or two more little houses to create an extended family enclave, with additions from both the eighteenth and nineteenth centuries. Toward the end of the nineteenth century, the houses were consolidated into a single dwelling that appeared much as the house does today—at least from the outside. When new owners acquired the property several years ago, they hired the esteemed French designer

Philippe Eckert, whose client list reads like a Who's Who of the wealthy, the royal, and the powerful, to redesign the interior and help landscape the exterior of their long-dreamt-of second home. Philippe worked closely with his clients, a couple who spend many months of the year in Provence and who favor contemporary art, clean lines, and neutral colors in their homes.

The kitchen was the special passion and personal project of the husband, who loves to cook. Says Philippe, "It was he who dictated the specifications and design elements in the kitchen. He wanted an uncluttered, pristine work

Opposite A collection of exotic spice bottles with brilliant red labels adds a dash of color to the neutral palette of this sleek country kitchen in a seventeenth-century restored village home in the Alpilles (*left*).

environment, a kitchen open to the dining room but still with a sense of two spaces. Specific elements he insisted on were two sinks, a La Cornue stove and oven, and shelves for a couple hundred cookbooks. A tranquil environment for cooking and dining was his ultimate goal."

In the house's original layout, there were two small rooms divided by an antique stone wall, where today the dining room and kitchen flow into each other. The entire center of the wall and the top half portion of the two sides were removed—not an easy undertaking when the wall is densely packed limestone more than a foot thick. With the wall transformed into two low dividers with a wide passage in between, the kitchen was ready for its makeover. Philippe created a sleek center island trimmed with wrought iron, where the home owner prepares his plates before serving. Philippe also designed the neat cream-colored cabinets: one set flanking a large marble sink, the other set built around the large stove. Cabinets on another wall, facing the sink, frame a La Cornue wall oven.

The husband does most of his food prep on a long butcher block countertop adjacent to the stove. The butcher-block top was designed with a small hole in the center to facilitate the disposal of trimmings into a garbage can placed below. All other countertops are in pale tiles of Votticino marble, bordered, like the butcher block island, in wrought iron. Open shelves on the wall adjacent to the stove are also of this tumbled marble trimmed in wrought iron. The same marble tiles the floor as well, enhancing the

Previous pages The kitchen's open cooking corner was designed around the La Cornue range for supreme practicality. The long workstation, covered in butcher block and bordered in wrought iron, features a discreet hole at one end for sweeping trimmings and peels into a small garbage can below. *Above* A carafe of chilled rosé wine, which the chef enjoys while preparing a meal, rests on a butcher block center island in front of a La Cornue wall oven framed by built-in cabinets. *Opposite* To the right of the range, a small marble sink stands ready for pot-filling or rinsing vegetables.

Looking out: Designer Philippe Eckert cut through a thick, centuries-old stone wall to open the kitchen to the beamed dining room. Now the chef can look out upon an imposing black-and-white painting by Leopoldo Maler and the walnut dining table where friends often gather for aperitifs.

kitchen with a harmony of texture and a soft, golden hue.

Much remains out of sight in this precisely designed and uncluttered domain. Most of the modern appliances, such as the dishwasher and the freezer, are ensconced in a large, well-lit *arrière-cuisine*, the "back kitchen" or pantry located behind the kitchen. Here the wines are stored, built-in cabinets hold serving platters and porcelain, and a large fridge is always generously stocked with champagne.

Decoration in the kitchen is minimal. The only spot of color comes from spice jars with brilliant red labels on a shelf near the stove. "My clients did not want many colors," says Philippe. "Rather, they preferred a neutral

palette of beige, cream, and stone. The house has a lot of contemporary art, so we kept the surroundings fairly simple to set off the art."

A dramatic, black-and-white painting by Dominican artist Leopoldo Maler dominates the heavily beamed dining room. An ornate crystal chandelier, a family heirloom, hangs above an early-twentieth-century walnut table surrounded by nineteenth-century slat-backed chairs. What catches your eye as you sit at the table gazing toward the kitchen is the owner's vast collection of cookbooks, whose titles reveal a passionate interest in food from every corner of the globe, from rustic fare to the cuisine of three-star Michelin chefs.

Looking in: For the owner, having his cookbooks on display was an important design element, as was the opulent crystal chandelier—a family heirloom—above the dining table. The small wood door next to the fireplace leads to a large pantry containing the dishwasher, the freezer, storage cabinets, and a large refrigerator stocked with champagne.

Beignets aux Abricots

SUGARED APRICOT DUMPLINGS

This is a delectable dessert for those few weeks of the year when fresh, ripe apricots are in season. Each apricot is stuffed with sugar, enrobed in a soft choux pastry, then boiled and finally coated with buttered bread crumbs and confectioners' sugar. Irresistible! Serve with a chilled sweet white wine such as a Beaumes de Venise or a Sauternes.

SERVES 4

For the choux pastry

½ cup milk

2 tablespoons unsalted butter, cut into bits

Fine sea salt

⅔ cup all-purpose flour

1 large egg

For the apricot dumplings

12 fresh apricots, whole, with pits carefully removed with a teaspoon or a grapefruit spoon

12 cubes turbinado (raw brown) or white sugar

6 tablespoons unsalted butter

¾ cup fresh bread crumbs

2 to 3 tablespoons confectioners' sugar

TO MAKE THE CHOUX PASTRY: In a medium saucepan, combine the milk, butter, and a pinch of salt. Bring to a boil over high heat, then remove from the heat and stir in the flour with a wooden spoon. Return to the heat and stir vigorously until the mixture thickens and starts to form a film on the bottom of the saucepan, about 1 minute. Remove from the heat and let cool for 3 to 4 minutes. Add the egg and beat vigorously with a whisk until blended and smooth. Set aside to cool to lukewarm.

TO MAKE THE APRICOT DUMPLINGS: Bring a large pot of water to a low boil over medium-high heat. While it heats, form the lukewarm dough into a log about 2 inches thick. Cut into twelve slices. Press the slices into 6-inch circles. Stuff a cube of sugar into the center of each apricot. Place an apricot in the center of each circle and bring the dough up and around the apricot so that it is completely enclosed. Press the edges to seal.

Using a slotted spoon, gently drop the dumplings into the boiling water, leaving enough space between each dumpling to allow it to expand. Cook at a low boil for 15 minutes, turning the dumplings frequently in the water to make sure they cook evenly. (You may have to do this in batches.) Again using a slotted spoon, transfer the dumplings to a wire rack (woven mesh style is ideal) to drain.

Meanwhile, melt the butter in a large skillet over medium heat. Add the bread crumbs and sauté, stirring frequently, until golden brown, 3 to 4 minutes. Remove the skillet from the heat and transfer the crumbs to a large plate. Roll the dumplings in the buttered bread crumbs to coat well. Arrange three dumplings on each of four serving dishes. Using a fine mesh strainer, dust confectioners' sugar over the dumplings and serve immediately.

Caroline's Spare and Luminous Cottage Kitchen

WHEN CAROLINE VOGELSANG came to this olive oil estate in the Alpilles region of Provence to visit friends several years ago, she fell in love with the property and decided she wanted it to be in her life always. When a small cottage-like apartment giving onto the courtyard in the property's former *grange* became available, Caroline snapped it up, and she has been renting it as a vacation retreat on a yearly basis for almost a decade. She decided to personalize the space and upgrade the amenities, with the wholehearted approval of the owners, shortly after she took on the apartment. She gutted the kitchen and re-created it as a space that is extremely simple and functional but very contemporary and stylish. It boasts handsome raw materials and an art lover's canny use of color as accent.

The apartment's original kitchen was in one of the small bedrooms, but Caroline wanted to create a large common room to share with friends. "I wanted a space with a lot of light," says Caroline, "so one of the first things I did was add a large square window over the sink. Light changes everything. For the basic design of the room, I wanted something unassuming, completely practical, wide open, and airy. I had shelves built in for storage, and used other existing

Opposite Small, thoughtful touches, such as a zinc pot of baby basil and green liquid dishwashing detergent stored in an old olive oil bottle, add style and personality to Caroline Vogelsang's apartment on the property of an olive-oil estate near Les Baux-de-Provence (*left*).

spaces for new purposes. The niche where the fridge is now was once arched and used for wood storage. I made the niches square. The work was done by the local mason, and the materials we used were very basic, mainly bricks and cement."

The kitchen floor is polished concrete, which Caroline had painted in a mottled sandstone beige for a less industrial look. The countertops and shelves are in a blue-gray cast concrete, although they were supposed to be a soft gray. "Unfortunately," remembers Caroline, "the color came out wrong, with a strong bluish cast. But I'm living with the color and slowly getting used to it."

Caroline added extremely simple elements to her décor as well as some rare *objets* that add éclat and surprise to the small space. One notable touch is the lighting. Caroline bought exterior patio lights from Habitat for the kitchen interior, and equipped them with a dimmer. She made another unusual choice for her curtains: "I didn't like the idea of curtains," she says, "but I needed something over the windows to dim the glaring afternoon light. On one of my trips to India I found bolts of a heavy, blue-bordered white cotton fabric favored by religious orders— very basic and beautiful. I bought many yards and had them stitched into simple panel curtains."

An *enfilade* of custom cast-concrete open shelves and storage niches holds a small stove, the dishwasher, and the double sink. The window over the sink was added to bring light into the back of the kitchen. The flooring is polished concrete painted in a mottled sandstone beige.

Above, left A whimsical and rare plate hand-painted in 1958 by Jean Cocteau at an atelier in Villefranche enjoys its own niche chez Caroline. *Above, right* Simple, blue-bordered cotton fabric from India filters late-afternoon sunlight. *Opposite* Pillows cover a cast-concrete base to form a cozy corner seating area. The low, rustic wood table in the foreground, which Caroline found at a flea market, is the room's all-purpose gathering spot, for breakfast, aperitifs, dinner, and general camaraderie, with guests sitting on a low sofa on one side or on large floor pillows.

Every detail of Caroline's little vacation abode has been thought through, down to the smallest, most prosaic element. Take the bottle for her dishwashing liquid, for example. "Dishwashing detergents come in very ugly bottles," she says, "and I didn't want ugliness in my kitchen. I loved the shape of the old olive oil bottle, and realized that with the classic pouring spout it would be a very practical container for the soap." Placed next to a little pot of basil on the windowsill above the sink, it makes a lovely small vignette, picking up the greens of the trees that shade the garden outside.

Sardines Escabèche

GRILLED FRESH SARDINES IN ESCABÈCHE MARINADE

An *escabèche*—composed of fried fish marinated and chilled in a tart mixture of lemon juice or vinegar with tomatoes or peppers, onions, herbs, and spices—is a popular dish in both Provence and Spain. Caroline uses fresh sardines, readily available in local Provençal markets, but you can substitute fillets of mackerel or whiting, or even slices of grouper or sea bass fillets. Serve this *escabèche* with lots of country bread to soak up the tasty sauce.

**SERVES 6 AS AN APPETIZER,
4 AS A MAIN COURSE**

3/4 cups all-purpose flour

Fine sea salt

Freshly ground black pepper

3 pounds fresh sardine fillets (12 to 16 sardines), cleaned, with heads and tails discarded

3 tablespoons extra-virgin olive oil

2 medium yellow onions, finely chopped

1 (28-ounce) can of peeled, crushed tomatoes

1 cup white wine vinegar

1 large sweet onion, such as Vidalia, coarsely chopped

3 garlic cloves, crushed, peeled, and coarsely chopped

1/3 cup chopped fresh flat-leaf parsley

1 cup fresh cilantro, leaves whole, with stems removed

Juice of two lemons

In a large bowl, combine the flour and generous pinches of salt and freshly ground pepper. Toss the sardine fillets in the flour until well coated. Set aside in the bowl. Just before frying, shake off excess flour from the fillets.

In a large skillet, heat the olive oil over medium-high heat. Add the yellow onions and sauté, stirring often, until soft and translucent but not browned, about 4 minutes. Add the sardine fillets and sauté (you may have to do this in two batches), turning once, until the fillets are golden brown and just cooked through, 1 to 2 minutes per side. Remove from the heat. Transfer the fillets to a large platter or baking pan lined with paper towels. Set aside.

Return the pan to medium-high heat. Add the tomatoes, vinegar, onion, garlic, and parsley, and season to taste with salt and pepper. Bring to a boil, then lower the heat to a simmer and cook the mixture, stirring frequently, until it thickens slightly and takes on the consistency of a light tomato sauce, about 20 minutes. Remove from the heat and cool to lukewarm.

Arrange half of the fish in a large, shallow earthenware or glass dish (ideally with a lid), and season with a bit more salt and pepper. Cover the fish with half of the tomato sauce, then sprinkle with half of the cilantro. Repeat the layering process with the remaining sardines and tomato sauce; reserve the remaining cilantro. Drizzle the lemon juice over the mixture, cover, and refrigerate for at least 6 hours or overnight. Remove the *escabèche* from the refrigerator about an hour before serving. Sprinkle with the remaining cilantro and serve.

A Touch of Glass:
A Mosaic Artist's
Atelier Kitchen

THE COOL, BLUE LIGHT of morning bathes the Paris duplex apartment of Pierre Mesguich, just as it did in 1909 when the space, then an artist's atelier, was occupied by Pablo Picasso. It was here that Picasso began his Cubist period, creating paintings such as *Girl with a Mandolin* and a series of portraits of his lover, Fernande Olivier. The apartment has evolved over the last century, changing functions and owners many times. Today the upper mezzanine level, with 18-foot ceilings and a view of Montmartre, serves as the living room and bedroom quarters, while the lower level, overlooking the courtyard, houses the kitchen and dining area. Says Pierre: "We wanted one large open space with no separation between the kitchen and the dining room, casual and welcoming for dinners with friends."

Pierre Mesguich is one of the world's most celebrated mosaic artists. He is sometimes referred to as the "Maestro of Mosaic," and his client list includes Prince Felipe of Spain, Paris designer Jean-Paul Gaultier, Sting, and the Hôtel Plaza Athénée in Paris. With these credentials, you might expect a blow-you-away mosaic wall dominating his own kitchen. Instead, the mosaic portion of Pierre's kitchen is confined to the backsplash, and was designed with subtlety and restraint. The

Opposite Pierre Mesguich designed the unique mosaic backsplash in his kitchen using hand-pressed, hand-cut vitreous glass-paste rectangles. *Left* A lavish nineteenth-century crystal chandelier adds a touch of grandeur to the pared down, contemporary ambience.

Previous pages Appliances covered in satin-finish stainless steel illuminate the windowless back area of the kitchen with reflected light from atelier windows overlooking a courtyard. Below the chandelier, a set of classic Philippe Starck "Pratfall" chairs in mahogany-veneered plywood with black leather seats surrounds the 1930s French mahogany and parchment table. *Above* Stainless-steel accents on the black granite countertop keep the look sleek and simple, catching the light as do the appliances, without distracting from the mosaic with any additional color. *Opposite, left* Open shelving that matches the tall bookshelves in the living room upstairs displays crystal stemware and serving pieces. *Opposite, right* A gently curved stairway leads to the upstairs living room. *Following pages, left* An easel poised by the atelier's tall windows displays 1930s period drawings of skiers discovered in a cellar storage room after Pierre purchased the apartment.

mosaic is composed of multicolored glass rectangles that are rich but muted in hue—olive, rust, mustard, and gray prevail. Pierre designs and produces the colored pieces from vitreous glass paste exclusively for each project. The glass is fired at 1,200 degrees Celsius, then hand-pressed and hand-cut. Patterns are sketched out on brown paper; the full-size drawing on which a design is based is called a "cartoon." The inspiration for his kitchen mosaic was twofold: "One inspiration," he says, "was a work by the Irish-born American abstract painter Sean Scully. The other, totally different, inspiration was an African textile I saw in Ghana."

Running beneath the backsplash, and fram-

ing the sink, is a countertop of black granite that Pierre refers to as "Zimbabwe stone." To make the old, chevron-patterned oak parquet floor more compatible with the anthracite-colored countertops, Pierre stained the floor a deep mahogany. Preferring open storage to cabinets, Pierre designed an *enfilade* of shelving that echoes the design of the tall bookshelves in the living room above. On the opposite wall, out of sight under winding stairs leading to the second-floor mezzanine, are the prosaic but essential appliances: a large refrigerator and freezer. Dotted along the ceiling, recessed spotlights illuminate the walls, hung with a series of Pierre's black-and-white photographs of family festivals and holidays. The walls, painted a soft gray-green, change in tone as the northern light waxes and wanes through the day.

A 1930s wood and parchment dining table surrounded by Philippe Starck Pratfall chairs is the physical focal point of the room, although the eye is constantly drawn to the mosaic. The table reinforces the room's almost geometric simplicity of design, but above it hangs a visual surprise—a nineteenth-century crystal chandelier from Saint-Germain-des-Prés antique dealer Ilse B. The chandelier's brilliantly cut crystal prisms and pendants refract the colors and pattern of Pierre's unique mosaic, a work with ancient antecedents but of purely contemporary beauty.

Meringues Géantes

OVERSIZE VANILLA MERINGUES

Easy to make, and impressive to serve, these crunchy oversize meringues are a perfect accompaniment to an assortment of fruit sorbets or a fresh mixed-berry salad. The only caution: Do not make these on a very hot, humid day. In sultry weather, the meringues can quickly lose their crunch and go limp. Garnish if you wish with lightly crushed toasted almonds. The meringues should keep for three or four days if stored at room temperature in an airtight container.

MAKES 6 TO 8 LARGE MERINGUES

1 cup egg whites (about 8 large)

1 cup granulated sugar

2 cups confectioners' sugar

1 teaspoon vanilla extract

$1/2$ cup sliced toasted almonds, lightly crushed (optional)

Preheat the oven to 200°F.

Line two baking sheets with lightly buttered parchment paper, buttered side up. Beat the egg whites with an electric mixer at medium speed until they begin to form soft peaks. Gradually add the granulated sugar, beating until the whites are stiff but not dry. Add the confectioners' sugar, passing the sugar through a strainer to keep it from clumping, and gently fold it in, a little at a time, with a rubber spatula. Add the vanilla extract and gently fold it in. Using a pastry bag, pipe six to eight meringues into circles about 4 inches wide and 3 inches high onto the baking sheet, spacing them about 1 inch apart. (You can also form the meringues freehand, using a large serving spoon to shape the meringue mixture into six to eight balls.) Sprinkle with sliced almonds if you wish.

Bake for $1^1/2$ to 2 hours, with the handle of a wooden spoon holding the oven door slightly ajar. Watch the meringues carefully as they bake; they should color to a pale beige and be crisp on the outside but slightly soft within. If the meringues begin to brown, lower the oven heat slightly. Transfer the baking sheet to a wire rack and cool the meringues. Set aside in a dry place (well away from steam or water) until ready to serve, or store in an airtight container.

CHEZ GHYSLAINE: AN ODE TO THE SIMPLE LIFE

NPRETENTIOUS, AIRY, and extremely practical, Ghyslaine Béguin's kitchen suits her house—and her personality—to perfection. In her classic *mas*, or farmhouse, surrounded by vineyards and woodland near Saint-Rémy-de-Provence, she wanted a comfortable, minimalist kitchen, full of light and very easy to maintain. No froufrou, not a lot of tiles and color, just functional and welcoming. Originally the kitchen's space was a storage garage for gardening tools—essentially an annex. (The original kitchen was a dark little room in the back of the house.) Ghyslaine wanted her kitchen open to the terrace and central to the house, ideally situated for receiving guests. The wrought-iron and glass kitchen door is now the main entrance to the house, and it is guarded

(benignly) by her eleven-year-old Labrador retriever, Paddock. "I wanted a place that was always 'elbows on the table,' both inside and outside on the terrace," she says. "Very relaxed, very *familiale*. My door is almost always open, literally, both to Paddock and to friends. I wanted there to be a real flow between inside and outside."

Ghyslaine designed her kitchen herself, and found a local contractor who could make her vision a reality. "I wanted everything in a straight line, no angles: the sink, the stove, the dishwasher, all lined up

Opposite Vivid touches of red—from the cheese bell to the teapot to the tomatoes—accent Ghyslaine Béguin's subdued gray and cream farmhouse kitchen. *Left* Just outside the kitchen door, the faithful yellow Labrador retriever, Paddock, greets visitors. (*Photo by Linda Dannenberg.*)

Ghyslaine prepares a casual weekend lunch. When friends come by for a meal, as they do several times a week, the table is set very simply with deep blue paper place mats and lavender paper napkins. Ghyslaine reserves her pressed vintage linens for special occasions. The stainless-steel hanging lamp above the table, an exterior patio fixture, hails from IKEA, while the little red hanging lamps in the background are by Tsé & Tsé.

in an *enfilade*," says Ghyslaine. "And I wanted little windows, with a shelf in between, to give light over the workspace." Emphasizing the linear flow are a long countertop and backsplash in a cool, gray, granite-like stone from Portugal (in French called *pierre de Portugal*). To keep the kitchen cool and as open as possible, a large second oven, as well as a freezer and a second refrigerator, ware set in a back room five steps below and behind the kitchen. During the hottest days

Shelving holds an assortment of clear and tinted glassware and a collection of brightly colored vintage-style breakfast bowls.

of summer, Ghyslaine carries her tarts and clafoutis down here to bake.

The tile work couldn't be more basic. "I chose very simple industrial white tiles, pure and plain," says Ghyslaine, "and tiled surfaces both seen and unseen. I like everything to be very clean, so I even had the inside of the cabinets tiled so mice couldn't penetrate the storage areas." The flooring also reveals a desire for simplicity and a bit of industrial inspiration. Instead of laying a traditional

terra-cotta tile floor, Ghyslaine opted for a gray floor of polished concrete—a choice becoming quite à la mode in French country houses. It helps keep the kitchen cool on the hottest dog days of summer, when the temperature can rise to about 110 degrees Fahrenheit.

Furniture in the kitchen is kept to a minimum—just the necessities—but handsome pieces those necessities are. An inlaid-wood extension table from Ghyslaine's family is surrounded by rush-seated chairs. The focal point of the room is on the windowless east wall: a gracefully carved nineteenth-century *buffet Provençal* in walnut, which Ghyslaine found at an antiques dealer in Arles. Above the buffet hangs a set of nineteenth-century *chromogravures*, prints of fruit and vegetable still lifes. Two small, red-shaded lamps from the cheeky Paris design firm Tsé & Tsé add sparks of color at the end of the countertop.

Outside on the kitchen's small terrace, where friends love to drop by for an aperitif on sultry evenings, an assortment of vintage garden chairs surrounds a unique, rather whimsical table sprung from Ghyslaine's imagination. On a long, rectangular wrought-iron base sits a thick, smooth slab of slate resembling a large blackboard, which indeed it often becomes. A little zinc pot next to the table holds brightly hued stubs of chalk, and the smooth surface is often covered with the colorful glyphs of Ghyslaine's young grandchildren, or scrawls from passing friends or family: "Bonjour, Maman!" . . . "Ciao, Ghyslaine" . . . "À tout à l'heure. . . ."

Above Two-year-old Alice, Ghyslaine's granddaughter, pauses during a hearty lunch to sip from an antique tumbler. (*Photo by Linda Dannenberg.*) *Opposite* A set of nineteenth-century *chromogravure* still-life prints adorns the wall above an antique walnut *buffet Provençal.* Always present on Ghyslaine's gleaming table is the graceful, flower-like wrought-iron hot plate, crafted in Arles by Gérard Péignon.

Clafoutis aux Fruits Rouges

RED-BERRY CLAFOUTI

A clafouti—similar to a flan—is beautiful in its simplicity, very easy to make, and impressive to serve. While clafoutis are typically mostly custard with a little bit of fruit, Ghyslaine's clafouti has an abundance of berries bound with soft custard—perfect for summer. You can make this berry-rich dessert with any assortment of blueberries, raspberries, fresh currants, blackberries, or ripe cherries that you find at the market. Just make sure the total volume of berries measures four cups. The clafouti, though delicious alone, is even more luscious with a spoonful of whipped cream on top.

SERVES 6 TO 8

6 large eggs

6 tablespoons granulated sugar

³/₄ cup half-and-half

6 tablespoons (²/₃ stick) unsalted butter, melted

6 tablespoons all-purpose flour

1¹/₂ cups blueberries

1¹/₂ cups raspberries

¹/₂ cup blackberries (if blackberries are unavailable, substitute another ¹/₂ cup raspberries)

¹/₂ cup ripe cherries, unpitted

1 rounded tablespoon confectioners' sugar

Preheat the oven to 400°F.

Butter a 10-inch round or 13 x 9-inch porcelain or glass baking dish, sprinkle with sugar, and set aside.

In the bowl of an electric mixer, or in a large mixing bowl, combine the eggs and granulated sugar and beat on medium until pale yellow and frothy. Beat in the half-and-half, butter, and flour and mix on medium until well blended and frothy.

Combine the blueberries, raspberries, blackberries, and cherries and spoon them into the bottom of the baking dish. Pour in the egg mixture. Bake in the center of the oven for 35 to 40 minutes, until the top is puffy and the custard surrounding the berries is golden brown. Remove to a wire rack to cool, 30 to 60 minutes. Using a fine-mesh strainer or a sifter, dust the top with confectioners' sugar and serve warm, as is or with a dollop of fresh whipped cream.

KITCHEN COLORS

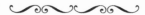

IN THE BEGINNING, THERE WAS THE WHITE KITCHEN, PURE AND SIMPLE. IN FACT, UNTIL THE MID-1900S, WHITE WAS THE PREDOMINANT INTERIOR COLOR IN MOST FRENCH COUNTRY HOMES. PARTICULARLY IN THE SOUTH OF FRANCE, WHITE WAS THE COLOR OF PURITY, cleanliness, and renewal. Renewal because, traditionally, once a year in the spring, home interiors were white-washed with an opaque mixture of lime, whiting, size, and water. (The lime killed any mildew, mold, or bacteria, so the walls were truly refreshed and purified.) In today's French country kitchens, white and its subtle variations—cream, ivory, and pearl—are still the hues of choice for kitchen walls. White reflects light and shows off other colors to advantage—in trim, tiles, and fabrics. White is the most versatile color: since it is achromatic, everything goes with it; nothing clashes. While the white- or cream-toned kitchen predominates in French country homes, I have visited a wide variety of kitchens decked in other colors, most in the yellow-ocher-peach spectrum.

Country kitchen yellows impart warmth, cheer, and welcome; they light up the kitchen with a sunny glow. More rare is the blue kitchen, many inspired by Monet's iconic blue-painted and blue-tiled kitchen at Giverny. Blue kitchens, however, come across as a little somber, both during the day and at night, and for this reason blue is not frequently chosen to embellish the kitchen's walls. What you also don't often see in France is a bright yellow-and-blue kitchen—another worn, clichéd image of French country style. You'll come across this impostor in decorating magazines featuring "French style," usually accessorized with ducks, roosters, hanging baskets, and vibrantly printed floral fabrics.

Where bright colors do come into play in the true French country kitchen is in the trim, the tile work, the furniture, and the accessories. I love kitchens with the pop of red. On a floor, a curtain, a chair, a shelf liner, or a set of vintage dish towels, red ignites a room. It plays well off of a white, soft yellow, or cream-tinted wall, or even a wall of palest blue. Juxtaposed with naturally finished cabinets or furniture of walnut, redwood, oak, cherry, and pine, red brings out the warmth of the patina and the grain.

I also like the grace and elegance of green, so long as it's muted, such as the soft, silvered green of olive leaves, or the grayed green of wild thyme, or the dusty green of almond trees. There is a particular green that I've seen often in Provence, used in the kitchen trim on beams or on furniture, that I love. It's a subtle green, softly blended with notes of gray and blue, and works handsomely in contrast with a cream-colored wall. Deeper greens—emerald or cypress, for example—may appear in tile work, alone in a monochromatic countertop or paired with ocher-yellow tiles in a harlequin-design backsplash.

The palette for Catherine Ligeard's classic country kitchen in the Luberon is cream and white, with accent colors coming from kitchen towels and checked curtains hiding the cookware beneath the countertops.

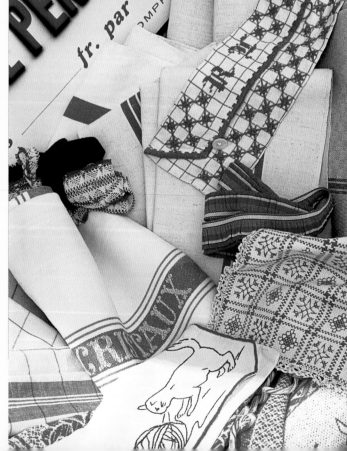

Clockwise from above A rosy Alsacian floral print fabric from Beauvillé adds cheer to a small kitchen shelf in Paris; a red-beaded curtain in a kitchen doorway allows air and filtered light in while keeping flies out; rush-seated chairs in many styles, such as this yellow fauteuil and red dining chair decorated with an olive motif, are a specialty of the Monleau firm in Vallabrèques; heavy beams painted in a traditional Provençal grayed green handsomely contrast with the buttercream hue of the kitchen walls; vintage towels, such as these at Au Petit Bonheur La Chance in Paris, often feature a touch of red.

Clockwise from above left Parsley green describes the tiled countertops of a château kitchen near Avignon; a blue *buffet-vaisselier* lends jaunty seaside style to a peach-hued kitchen on the Île-de-Ré; a collection of eighteenth-century earthenware crocks adds a glow to a Paris kitchen; blue-and-white Provençal linens and plates dress up the table in a cream-colored dining room in the Luberon; this sophisticated kitchen in the Île-de-France, with walls the color of vanilla custard and chair cushions adding a discreet touch of blue, once housed the waterwheel of a seventeenth-century mill.

A touch of blue adds elements of class, and understated charm to a kitchen. Blue most frequently makes an appearance in the decorative design of sparkling tile work, usually blue on white, with a provenance of Holland (Delft), France, or Morocco. It is also widely used in curtains, tablecloths, seat cushions, and collections of blue-glazed pottery, as in cream-colored Provençal kitchen I know in Goult, where almost every accessory is touched with blue. Blue can also play a more dominant role, as I observed in a kitchen in Saint-Rémy-de-Provence, where the custom-made cabinets were stained in a Prussian blue inspired by a collection of vintage blue-enameled coffee pots. Wherever and however color is used in the best French country kitchens, it is used with imagination, discretion, and taste.

RUSTIC COUNTRY

THE WARM, RUSTIC KITCHEN that celebrates all things country is one of the most welcoming and soul-stirring of all French rooms. Imbued with the spirit of a farmhouse, a rough-and-tumble post house, or a rural cottage lost in time, the rustic kitchen sets everyone at ease. Colors can be vibrant, enhanced by state-of-the-art lighting, as in a kitchen crafted from a former coach house, or simply hues of natural wood and stone, lighted only by candles, as in a pond-side cottage in the Berry region. The atmosphere is always warm and relaxed. Objects can be purchased from antiques dealers, picked up for a song at barn sales and salvage lots, or—what luck!—discovered in the wine cellar of an old family property. However the rustic kitchen may come together, it exudes an unpretentious charm that is extremely seductive. ❧

VIBRANT PROVENÇAL IN AN ANTIQUE STABLE

CRAFTED INTO THE FRAMEWORK of a seventeenth-century stable, once part of a grand château in the Petite Camargue village of Saint-Laurent-d'Aigouze, this warm and personal ocher-hued kitchen pays homage both to the traditions of place and to family history. It is an amalgam of Provençal, Napoleon III, and contemporary trends from the south of France. A preponderance of dark metal—wrought and cast iron in the stove hood, in border trim along the countertops, and in cabinet and door frames—gives the kitchen a distinctive masculine edge, augmented by the speckled black polished-concrete countertops. The metal accents and masculine air hark back to the stable's role as an ancient *relais*, a post house for passing coaches

with a blacksmith's forge on premises. Today the *relais* is a stylish, comfortable village house, La Maison de Dalame, home to retired businessman Daniel Léonhardt.

To create his kitchen, Daniel demolished the walls of the stable in order to open it onto the stone-walled terrace, where he installed his pool. Veranda doors open directly onto the pool—partially covered by a timbered ceiling and partially open to the sky—which Daniel added to illuminate the kitchen with the water's reflected light. "Houses in the area weren't originally

Opposite Warmth emanates from the kitchen of Daniel Léonhardt's former coach house near Aigues-Mortes thanks to the "flushed yellow" of the walls and the active antique fireplace, where seasoned wood is always at hand. *Left* An inner courtyard offers this village home privacy and calm.

designed with many windows," notes Daniel, "because the houses would get too hot in the summer with the midday sun heating the interiors through any aperture. The idea was to keep light out most of the day. Today we prefer rooms filled with light." To brighten the room further, the heavily beamed ceiling and the moldings are painted a bright creamy white.

The unusual amount of dramatic metalwork accents in his kitchen was inspired, Daniel says, by the houses in which he and his father grew up near Lyon. These were prestigious bourgeois dwellings built early in the industrial revolution, when many windows and doorways were generously trimmed in metal, a design element that truly came into its own during the mid-1800s. À la mode were grand verandas composed of metal—iron or zinc—and glass, a dramatic form whose function was to welcome and enhance the light. To retard rusting and tarnishing of his extensive metalwork, Daniel uses the old-fashioned method of polishing the metal surfaces with a paste of beeswax. The polished-concrete countertops, stained black, also get their gleam from beeswax, which Daniel heats before applying.

Although the kitchen's contemporary flooring is Moroccan, the cement tiles that compose the pattern recall another trend from the late nineteenth century, when

Bold wrought-iron trim bordering the polished concrete countertops and framing the glass doors and cabinets endows Daniel's kitchen with a distinctly masculine air. The large steel-clad range is the Paul Bocuse model by Rosières.

Above, left White coco beans soak before cooking atop an unlit burner of the Rosières range. *Above, right* An historic cupboard that once graced the legendary Lyon restaurant La Mère Brazier, closed years ago, is now one of Daniel's prized possessions. *Opposite* A young visitor enjoys a swim in the pool, where he can be observed both from the kitchen, which opens onto the pool, and from a seat on the terrace.

cement tiles were all the rage in the south of France. The tiles in the Léonhardt kitchen are more subtle than the complexly patterned and colored cement creations made around Aix-en-Provence during the Belle Époque; here, a muted beige tone predominates, bordered by a band of graphic striped tiles in grays, browns, rust, and ocher. Adding a subtle harmony to the room, the same beige tiles that cover the floor also form the tall diagonally set backsplash behind the large Paul Bocuse model range by Rosières.

The ocher strip picks up the color of the kitchen's yellow walls: "yellow flushed with a little red" is how Daniel describes it. It was a color he and his fiancée loved, one they'd

seen and admired in the pages of *Côté Sud* magazine, the bible of Provençal style. "We had the paint specially mixed at a shop in Avignon," recalls Daniel. "The paint is a custom blend of *chaux*, a lime-based color wash, mixed with acrylics. The combination creates a more durable paint that can be washed and maintained but still has a traditional Mediterranean lime-wash look."

Completing the kitchen composition chez Léonhardt is a massive Portuguese marble double sink found in a flea market in Lyon; a vintage brick and stone fireplace from the Beaujolais region ("A kitchen should always have a working fireplace," Daniel says, "to give life to the room"); and cabinet doors of translucent glass. The one piece of furniture in the kitchen ensemble most beloved by Daniel stands just outside the kitchen proper, taking pride of place in the center hallway. It is a historic cupboard originally built in the early 1900s for the German consulate in Lyon. After World War II, it was bought for the legendary Lyon restaurant La Mère Brazier, where it remained for more than half a century until the restaurant closed and all its effects were sold by descendants of Madame Brazier several years ago. "It was just a stroke of luck, and a good connection, that brought this wonderful piece of furniture, full of memories, home to me," says Daniel, proud son of Lyon.

Calmars à la Dalame

SAUTÉED CALAMARI PROVENÇAL

This rustically simple and delicious recipe for squid demands top-quality ingredients—the freshest squid, prepared by your fishmonger, and high-quality extra-virgin olive oil—for the best results. Daniel Léonhardt serves this dish with short-grain white rice from the Camargue region of Provence and a dry white wine.

SERVES 6

¼ cup extra-virgin olive oil

6 medium yellow onions, thinly sliced

Fine sea salt

Freshly ground black pepper

2 pounds fresh squid (calamari), cleaned and sliced into bite-sized pieces

½ teaspoon Tabasco sauce, or to taste

In a large skillet, heat the olive oil over medium heat. Add the onions, season lightly with salt and pepper, and cook, stirring frequently, until the onions are soft and translucent but not browned, 4 to 5 minutes. Increase the heat to high, add the squid pieces, stir to coat with the oil, and sauté, stirring often, just until the calamari turn white and start to snap, crackle, and pop, 1 to 2 minutes. Do not overcook or the calamari will become rubbery. Remove from the heat, add the Tabasco sauce and salt and pepper to taste, and toss to combine. Serve immediately.

Chic-Rustique: A Decorator's Farmhouse Kitchen

PARIS DECORATOR Marie-José Pommereau is known for her refined sense of style and her formal décors inspired by aristocratic eighteenth-century homes, many commissioned for the Hôtel Plaza Athénée. But when she bought and restored an old property near Saint-Rémy-de-Provence as a second home, casual country style was her own mandate. She created her gracious Provençal retreat out of a rustic but structurally nondescript eighteenth-century farmhouse that was almost in ruins. The kitchen and dining area, originally the farmhouse's only common room, had been "disfigured," as Marie-José puts it, divided into three small rooms and painted in psychedelic colors. Lovingly transformed over two years, the house today is endowed

with a predominantly gray and beige palette, and has the air of a family home passed down through generations. Marie-José's love of subtle textures, subdued colors, and period furniture informs every inch of the space.

Marie-José set out her priorities: "I wanted a luminous, comfortable, warm, and luxurious home," she explains. "Luminous from light flooding in from added doors and windows. Comfortable and warm, so that the house would be a happy environment for family and friends. And luxurious, achieved through fine fabrics

---

Opposite In the farmhouse kitchen of decorator Marie-José Pommereau, a large *meuble de métier,* or artisan's work table, serves as an island for culinary prep work as well as a divider between the large room's two functions: cooking and dining. *Left* The dining area offers cozy seating for aperitifs or coffee.

and materials—simple perhaps, but of good quality, and always with interesting details."

Marie-José didn't want a classic, self-contained kitchen, but rather an open family room with a dining table and cozy armchairs in front of the stone fireplace. "I had found a large *meuble de métier*—an artisan's worktable almost ten feet long—at an antiques dealer's, and I imagined this as the 'island' divider between the two functions of the room: cooking and dining. I added slatted shelves under the top for storage." The beamed and slatted ceiling, original to the house, unites the space, as does the unusual stone-tiled floor painted ocher red more than a hundred years ago to resemble terra-cotta tiles. Much of the paint has worn off, giving the floors a dappled look. "Most people when they renovate refinish floors like this, bringing them back to their natural stone," says Marie-José, "but I loved the faded red look."

Many other vintage elements, which Marie-José found at flea markets and antique shops throughout the south of France, blend seamlessly into the new ensemble as well, as if they had coexisted for generations. The nineteenth-century pink marble sink, for example, was salvaged from a house in Bordeaux. Marie-José discovered the large nineteenth-century cupboard that commands one wall of the dining room while strollling the antiques shops in L'Isle-sur-la-Sorgue the day after she moved into her house. "Finding

Under rough-hewn, whitewashed beams, a variety of chairs and a *canapé* circle Marie-José's dining table. Nothing matches but everything is in harmony.

Above, left In the pantry, a large vintage *garde-manger* with its original hardware and screened doors that aerate the shelves stores provisions the old-fashioned way. *Above, right* The dining table sports an unusual *art populaire*, or folk art, base with legs carved to resemble tree trunks. *Opposite* A stroke of luck guided Marie-José to the nineteenth-century cupboard that stretches along the wall behind the dining table; its proportions and style suited the space as perfectly as if it had been made to order.

it was a real stroke of luck," she exclaims. "It was the perfect size and exactly the look that I was seeking." Facing the cupboard is an antique *art populaire* dining table with unusual legs carved to resemble slim tree trunks. Above it hangs a Spanish wrought-iron chandelier—electrified but always kept very dim at night since Marie-José prefers her table awash in candlelight.

The kitchen gives onto a pantry where a vintage *garde-manger*—a large, screen-doored cabinet designed for keeping cheeses, bread, and vegetables—holds pride of place. "I bought it just because I found it pretty, with-

Discovered almost in ruins, Marie-José's eighteenth-century farmhouse near Saint-Rémy-de-Provence was carefully restored over two years. In addition to bringing the house back to life, Marie-José also created the lawns and gardens, adding a swimming pool and several large trees for shade.

out really knowing where I would use it," says Marie-José, "but in fact it's proved to be very practical in here, doing exactly what it was meant to do." Other elements in Marie-José's kitchen are found objects with character, and have been put to other uses than their original function. An old wrought-iron garden gate, for example, bought years ago and stored away, eventually found its new raison d'être as an undersink cabinet door, camouflaging pipes and cleaning products with its elegant grillwork. Intriguing vintage detritus combined with imagination yields distinctive style, particularly in the projects of Marie-José Pommereau.

Tian de Légumes Provençal

GRATIN OF EGGPLANT, TOMATOES, AND RED ONION

"*Tian*" refers to a rustic, traditional Provençal baked side dish or main course, as well as to the heavy oven-proof earthenware dish in which it is made. The ingredients for this vegetable *tian*, a dish that Marie-José often serves, are simply assembled, drizzled with olive oil, and baked.

SERVES 6

2 medium eggplants (a long, slim shape is preferable), about 1 pound each, ends trimmed, sliced into ½-inch rounds

2 pounds ripe plum tomatoes, sliced into ½-inch-thick rounds

3 garlic cloves, peeled and finely sliced

2 tablespoons chopped fresh thyme leaves

1 tablespoon chopped fresh rosemary

1 bay leaf

5 tablespoons extra-virgin olive oil

Fine sea salt

Freshly ground black pepper

1 large red onion, sliced into ½-inch-thick rounds

2 tablespoons coarsely chopped flat-leaf parsley

Preheat the oven to 425°F. Combine the eggplants, tomatoes, garlic, thyme, rosemary, and bay leaf in a bowl. Pour in 3 tablespoons of the olive oil and toss lightly. Season to taste with salt and pepper and toss again. Turn the mixture into a 10-inch ovenproof earthenware or porcelain baking dish. Scatter the red onion slices over the top.

Bake in the center of the oven for 15 minutes, then reduce the heat to 350°F and bake for another 45 minutes, or until the vegetables are browned and slightly wilted. Sprinkle with the chopped parsley, drizzle with the remaining 2 tablespoons of olive oil, and serve either hot or at room temperature.

A Cottage Kitchen Equipped
with Candlelight and Charm

P ARIS DECORATOR ÉRIC CHAILLOUX spends his weekends far from the madding crowd in a rustic cottage with no electricity or running water. Located in the central Berry region, the cottage was once a small stable for horses on the property of a grand estate. A decade ago, Éric transformed the stable into a quirky and beguiling little cottage, full of modest antiques and finds from flea markets, auctions, and architectural salvage firms. "I wanted simplicity in my lifestyle here," says Éric, "but I still wanted to be surrounded by some vintage comforts—old silver, crystal, artisans' benches and tables full of character, and an eighteenth-century Louis XVI fireplace mantel."

The original stable was a simple rectangular structure.

Éric built on a small wing of stone for his kitchen. The project was rather labor intensive, since Éric gathered the stones himself all around the region—from his garden, in nearby woods, or wherever he happened to be. Most of the elements in the kitchen are humble finds, such as a simple, sturdy woodworker's table almost ten feet long, a nineteenth-century bistro table, and a flea-market étagère to hold pots and pans. Other items, though, work in elegant counterpoint to the rusticity: an eighteenth-century-inspired chandelier in iron that Éric designed for the space, an ornate sculpted wood chair with a fringed

Opposite Humble but stylish flea-market furnishings meet romantic candlelight— essential since there is no electricity. *Left* Once a stable, Éric Chailloux's cottage retreat in Berry charms visitors with its stone walls,

seat, and an enormous mirror (once part of an exhibit at the Palais de Tokyo in Paris) that covers one wall, doubling the kitchen's light and sense of space.

"I don't allow any plastic in here," says Éric. "I try to keep all the elements in natural materials—wood, metal, stone, glass. I became very ecologically aware almost by accident. I didn't want to leave big plastic sacks of garbage to be picked up when I was away. So I started bringing food home in cardboard cartons or paper bags that could be burned in the fireplace. Leftover food and peelings I put into a compost heap. There is almost no garbage. And I—and all of my friends who come to visit—have learned to appreciate and conserve water. All my water comes from a well, so we need to go outside, pump what we need, and bring it back in." What about toilets? you might well ask. Don't. There are none, at the moment. Think backwoods camping. . . .

"Once they get over their trepidation at the lack of modern conveniences, my friends love it here," says Éric. "After a two- or three-day visit, they don't even think about it anymore. They are enchanted in the evening in a house romantically lit only by candlelight, and dinners cooked by an open fire." Living a nineteenth-century life in the twenty-first

An enormous mirror on the kitchen's back wall doubles the room's natural light from a facing window and enhances its sense of space. Éric designed the eighteenth-century-inspired wrought-iron chandelier, the kitchen's main source of light in the evening when guests gather for dinner at the nineteenth-century bistro table.

Above A vast carpenter's table almost 10 feet long stands in as a countertop and serving station, while an old étagère bolted to the wall above holds pots and pans.
Opposite Framing the doorway into the kitchen, the living room's ornate trompe l'oeil paneling contrasts starkly with the kitchen's rough stone walls, which Éric constructed by himself, stone by stone.

century—one free of computers, television, radio, and electric bills—makes for a delightful weekend and vacation escape, but as a year-round lifestyle, Éric acknowledges, it would be impossible. His sophisticated, professional life in Paris makes him appreciate his unique retreat in Berry all the more, since his days there are few and precious, and far from the quotidian.

Pommes de Terre Boulangères en Croûte

"BAKER'S WIFE" POTATOES IN A PASTRY CRUST

This delicious free-form tart is a variation of the classic French potato dish *pommes de terre à la boulangère,* or "baker's wife potatoes," originally a mixture of potatoes and cheese baked in the always-hot baker's oven. Éric serves this tart as a hearty side dish to a roast beef, or as a nice Sunday supper accompanied by a big green salad and a hearty red wine.

SERVES 6 TO 9

3 tablespoons unsalted butter

1 large onion, very thinly sliced

$^3/_4$ cup crème fraîche

$^1/_2$ cup chopped curly leaf parsley

Fine sea salt

Freshly ground black pepper

$^1/_4$ teaspoon ground nutmeg

2 (9$^1/_2$-inch square) sheets commercial puff pastry

2 pounds medium russet potatoes, parboiled for 10 minutes, peeled, and sliced into $^1/_8$-inch-thick rounds

1 egg, lightly beaten, for glazing

In a medium skillet, melt the butter over medium heat. Add the onions, stir to coat with the butter, and cook, stirring frequently, until the onions are just translucent, about 3 minutes. Remove from the heat and set aside.

In a medium bowl, combine the crème fraîche, parsley, a pinch of salt and pepper, and nutmeg and stir to blend. Set aside.

Preheat the oven to 400°F.

On a lightly floured work surface, lay out one sheet of puff pastry. Roll out in a rectangle 12 inches by 10 inches; repeat with the other sheet. Set one sheet aside.

Arrange an overlapping layer of half of the potatoes across one sheet of pastry, leaving a 1-inch border on all sides. Spread half of the crème fraîche mixture over the potatoes, and scatter the cooked onions on top. Arrange the remaining potatoes on top, followed by the remaining crème fraîche mixture. Lay the second puff pastry sheet over the potato mixture, aligning its edges with the bottom sheet. Press the edges of the two pastry sheets together to seal, then fold them to the underside of the tart. Brush the top of the tart with the egg glaze. With a sharp knife, score two lines down the center of the tart about 1 inch apart, taking care not cut all the way through the dough. Along the right side of the tart, cut four small diagonal slits about $^3/_4$ inch wide into the pastry, this time cutting completely through the dough. Repeat along the left side. These are ventilation holes. Transfer the tart to a baking sheet.

Bake the tart in the center of the oven for 30 minutes. Reduce the heat to 350°F and bake for another 30 minutes, until the crust is a rich golden brown. (If the crust starts to get too dark after 45 minutes or so, cover lightly with a sheet of aluminum foil and continue baking.) Cool the tart on a wire rack for 20 minutes. Slice into six 4 x 5-inch pieces for a main-course serving, or cut smaller squares as a side dish, and serve.

Mas de Barbut:
A Collectible-Lover's
Kitchen

BRIMMING WITH POTTERY and culinary *objets*, this long, narrow kitchen, a relatively new addition to a house dating from the seventeenth century, reflects a great passion and respect for the past. Both owner Danielle Gandon and her mother were born in this house west of Montpellier, and family history on the property, which was once a wine-producing estate, extends back four generations. When Danielle and her husband, Jean-Claude, returned to the family domain in 1995 after seven years in Mexico, creating a new kitchen was a priority.

They knew they wanted the space to have good light, and a décor showcasing mostly vintage materials. Their design was founded on three key elements: a trove of two-hundred-year-old glazed tiles

found in a forgotten wine cellar; a broad but shallow eighteenth-century stone sink that had been in the house's original kitchen; and a tall *buffet à deux corps* (chest-on-chest), a family heirloom from the Cévennes region. "I wanted to use as many old original elements and salvaged elements as possible," says Danielle. "We started with what we had, and built from them. We put in a traditional *cheminée*, the fireplace, surrounded by a classic *potager*, with little "soup-warmer" plaques and round holes to hold pots over the embers. Then we surrounded the whole area with the beautiful yellow,

---

Opposite At the Mas de Barbut (*left*), a vine-covered bed-and-breakfast in the Petite Camargue, antique glazed tiles, terra-cotta roofing tiles, and a vast collection of decorative pottery from France and Mexico reflect Danielle Gandon's passion for ceramics.

green, and brown tiles from the wine cellar. We designed a wall to accommodate the *buffet à deux corps*, setting it into a shallow niche, and then centered the heavy old stone sink under a pair of French windows."

With this trinity of period elements in place, the Gandons composed the rest of the kitchen around them, keeping the traditional and the authentic foremost in their minds. The kitchen's space was cobbled together by combining a *grange*, or storage barn, and a *bergerie*, or sheepfold. The original stones of the antique arches, dating from the seventeenth century, come from the *bergerie*, and are highlighted now in the kitchen's architecture. A new outside wall, the only one that could accommodate windows, was designed to bring a maximum of light into the kitchen, with a large oval *oeil-de-boeuf*, or bull's-eye window, set above the French windows.

The handsome wine-cellar tiles that adorn the fireplace niche also cover the countertops and the backsplash. Wrought-iron edgings define the counter's linear stretch. The vintage mottled terra-cotta tile floor has an interesting provenance as well. The tiles, found at a salvage house, were originally used as roofing tiles, in the flat layer of support tiles that run under the roof's traditional canal tiles. Here these humble flat terra-cotta tiles have come down in the world, from the roof to the floor.

Guests at the Mas de Barbut take breakfast and sometimes dinner at a long harvest table, set between an heirloom chest-on-chest from the Cévennes and the fireplace, which is clad with two-hundred-year-old glazed tiles from an old wine cellar. Antique stones from a seventeenth-century sheepfold are incorporated into the back wall.

Above A cupboard presents a collection of brown
earthenware platters and bowls from Mexico and France.
Opposite, left An immense and heavy eighteenth-century
stone sink, part of the estate's original kitchen, was set in
place along the tiled windowsill to have the benefit of
maximum light. The sink's very shallow basin, called a *pile*
in this area of southern France, is normally used for
washing vegetables and fruit, but here makes an attractive
surface for displaying some of Danielle's favorite pottery
pieces, including an antique green-glazed colander from
Provence. *Opposite, right* To bring as much light as possible
into the kitchen, the Gandons added a large, round *oeil-de-
boeuf,* or bull's-eye, window, set into the kitchen's thick
outside wall above a traditional French window.

As in other kitchens I've seen where a traditional, old-fashioned look was sought, most
modern conveniences have been installed out
of sight in an *arrière-cuisine,* or back kitchen.
Here the dishwasher, oven, refrigerator, and
freezer keep to themselves behind a wooden
door. The kitchen's one modern element—
the range—has been camouflaged, its steel
surfaces refaced with antique iron doors and
antique tile work.

Danielle is a passionate collector, always
on the lookout for ceramics or vintage
kitchen items. She most treasures examples
of culinary pottery and popular-crafts pottery. Her vast collection comprises hundreds
of pieces, including the faience of four generations that she found tucked away in attics
and old kitchens in the region. The kitchen is
dense with decorative pottery, both vintage

Provençal pieces and Mexican pottery collected during the years that the Gandons spent living in Mexico. The vintage light fixture that hangs above the harvest table is a traditional billiards room fixture that once illuminated a billiards table. Danielle exchanged the original dark green shades for a trio of pale-hued unmatched shades, and hung it with colorful glass *photophores*, little lanterns that hold votive candles, a transformation that endows the fixture with a bit of whimsy and romance. The chairs around the dining table are a motley assortment—two green chairs coming from Mexico, the others from the old house or flea-market finds.

The creation of the kitchen was a joint project with her husband, Danielle explains, and a labor of love. "I imagined and con-ceived the design and décor," she says, "inspired by my three existing elements. Jean-Claude, who totally understood my vision, took over from there and built every inch of the kitchen from scratch." Today the couple works in tandem on another joint project: they have opened their home, Le Mas de Barbut, as a bed-and-breakfast inn, with three romantic bedrooms. Guests enjoy breakfast at the harvest table in the kitchen, or outside at tables under the spreading fig tree. Three nights a week, Danielle offers a table d'hôte, a single prix-fixe menu with offerings of savory rustic fare, such as her sautéed tuna in wine marinade, and a variety of baked vegetable *tians*, or casseroles. Danielle and Jean-Claude's neighbors and friends, as well as their guests, reserve well ahead for these popular feasts.

Thon Mariné

SAUTÉED TUNA IN WINE MARINADE

This easy, tender tuna dish is ready to serve in less than fifteen minutes. While the fish does not marinate in the sauce before cooking, the sweet-and-sour marinade that bathes the tuna at the end of the cooking time enhances the savory rich flavor of the fish. Danielle serves the tuna with roasted potatoes or a potato-and-tomato casserole (pictured below) dotted with garlic, drizzled with olive oil, and sprinkled with herbs.

SERVES 4

⅓ cup (5 tablespoons) extra-virgin olive oil

4 (½-pound) tuna steaks

Fine sea salt

Freshly ground black pepper

2 large sweet onions, such as Vidalia, thinly sliced

¾ cup red wine vinegar

3 tablespoons sugar

In a large skillet, heat 3 tablespoons of the olive oil over medium heat. Season the tuna steaks with salt and pepper, then add them to the pan. Sauté until lightly browned on one side, about 2 minutes, then turn and cook on the other side another 2 minutes. Using a slotted spatula, remove the tuna to a plate and set aside.

Add the remaining 2 tablespoons of olive oil to the skillet and heat over medium heat. Add the onions and sauté, stirring frequently, until the onions are translucent but not browned, 4 to 5 minutes. Add the vinegar and sugar, season to taste with salt and pepper, and stir to combine. When the mixture reaches a simmer, return the tuna to the skillet and cook, basting the fish frequently with the sauce, for about 5 minutes.

Using a slotted spatula, transfer a tuna steak to each of four serving plates, top with onions from the pan, then spoon the sauce over each serving. Serve immediately.

FURNISHING THE KITCHEN

THE FRENCH COUNTRY KITCHEN IS A DISTINCTIVE AND INSPIRING ROOM THAT REPRESENTS THE SUM OF MANY PARTS. ONE OF ITS MOST DISTINCTIVE ATTRIBUTES IS THE PREDOMINANCE OF FREESTANDING FURNITURE AS OPPOSED TO BUILT-IN CABINETRY. THE GRACEFUL and functional French furniture created for the kitchen over the last couple of centuries—such as the *vaisselier* or *buffet-vaisselier* for storing glassware, the *panetière* for storing bread, the *garde-manger* for cool storage behind screens or grillwork, and the étagère for displaying and storing dishes or glassware—is just one of the components that adds much charm to these rooms.

In many French country kitchens, the one piece of furniture that commands center stage is the kitchen table. Often it functions both as a place for dining and as a workstation in the absence of a center island. An iconic table, and one of the most popular for the kitchen as well as the dining room, is the long, rustic farm or harvest table.

The tables, antique or contemporary, which seat eight to fourteen, often with cutlery drawers at the ends, can be in honey-toned walnut, cherry, pine, or other woods, and even in stone. Chairs around the table are frequently a motley assortment of flea-market finds. A top choice in new chairs is the rush-seated variety, practical and perfect for a country vibe. Refectory-style benches are also an option for farm-table seating. Another eye-catching table is one with a thick marble top and elaborate cast-iron legs, a large version of the classic bistro table. Marble-topped tables function handsomely as work areas; the surface is particularly well-suited to pastry making.

Attractive kitchen storage is the raison d'être of the *buffet-vaisselier,* a buffet cabinet with doors and/or drawers topped by a recessed wooden étagère to hold dishes and glassware. The open shelves of the étagère often have a decorative bar or a strip of spindles that prevents the dishes from sliding out.

The *encoignure* is a corner buffet cabinet with doors on the bottom and display shelves on top. The kitchen corner is often forgotten territory, and the *encoignure,* a piece that is usually painted with an antique finish (if not a true antique), takes full advantage of its possibilities. Another attractive, usually antique, piece of furniture that offers ample storage is the *garde-manger,* a food storage cabinet crafted to somewhat resemble an armoire but with an openwork façade punctuated with wooden grillwork or spindles that allow air to pass through. Sometimes the open area is covered by screens rather than grillwork. The *garde-manger* was designed to store cheeses, root vegetables, dried sausages, jams, and cooling cakes and tarts—a function that it still performs admirably,

Unmatched but compatible chairs unified by blue-and-white Souleiado cushions surround a sturdy nineteenth-century farm table in the kitchen of an estate near Rambouillet.

Left An antiques shop in L'Isle-sur-la-Sorgue offers unusual furniture pieces created for the Provençal kitchen—a lavishly carved eighteenth-century *pétrin,* once used for kneading and proofing dough, and, displayed on top, a quaint *salière,* or lidded saltbox, right, and a cutlery holder called a *coutelière. Above, left* A long dining table inset with *pierre de Tavel,* polished stone from the northern Rhône Valley, highlights the kitchen of antiques dealer and designer Bruno Carles. *Above, right* Just-washed greens and edible blossoms rest on the thick marble top of a nineteenth-century bistro table in a Provençal kitchen. *Opposite, above left* A nineteenth-century *buffet à deux corps* reinterprets eighteenth-century motifs in its painted décor. *Opposite, above right* A dramatically carved *encoignure* (corner cabinet) adds architectural interest to the small kitchen of decorator Nono Girard. *Opposite, below right* A dainty, decorative *encoignure,* patinated in a mottled lime green, has an altar-like presence in a Luberon kitchen.

should you be lucky enough to find an eighteenth- or nineteenth-century original at an antiques fair.

Beyond these classic pieces of kitchen-inspired furniture, French home owners and designers become very creative in outfitting their kitchens. Pieces that were never intended to keep company with a stove, such as salvaged library shelving or a pharmacist's cabinet, are restored and adapted for the kitchen to hold earthenware platters, pitchers and plates, and mustards, jams, and sugars. A nineteenth-century carpenter's bench in one kitchen I saw, and a turn-of-the-twentieth-century fabric cutter's table in another, do yeoman duty as unique center islands. With imagination and an open mind, you can find treasures while scouring a flea market or an antiques

Above A half-wall inset with a window separates the kitchen from the dining room in an antique Burgundy farmhouse. *Opposite, above left* A tall nineteenth-century Provençal *buffet a deux corps* displays a twinkling collection of crystal decanters and other vintage glassware in a sumptuous kitchen near Gordes. *Opposite, above right* At the home of antiques dealers and designers Claude and Alain Fassier in the Perche, a long wall of shallow built-in cabinets with sliding glass doors is painted a dusty blue, while the interior, painted a dramatic garnet, boldly displays crystal stemware and porcelain terrines. The Frassiers chose a well-worn artisan's table for dining, with a top bearing hammer marks and multiple indentations from a vise. *Opposite, below right* The sensuous curves of eighteenth-century Provencal furniture design echo in the graceful lines of an Avignon pied-à-terre's open shelving.

fair that will make your kitchen strikingly original as well as entirely practical. Among the richest sources for intriguing antiques is the Sunday flea market, and the surrounding permanent antiques dealers, of L'Isle-sur-la-Sorgue, in Provence. Many homes in these pages boast treasured antique furniture and accessories found in its stalls and shops.

Customized built-in storage is not the norm in the traditional French country kitchen, but when it is used, it is likely to feature open, étagère-style shelving. The best examples take into consideration the space, the style of the kitchen, and the period of the house; they show imagination and originality; and, when appropriate, they acknowledge the past. A tiny apartment kitchen in Avignon, no larger than a closet, is not with-

out style thanks to the elegant design details of three long shelves. In the simple white kitchen of an antique farmhouse in Burgundy, plain shelving in an alcove next to the refrigerator derives visual interest not so much from the shelves themselves but from the colorful assortment of collectibles. And in the Île-de-France, the owner of a large nineteenth-century village house created a wall of shallow cabinets in his kitchen, with sliding glass doors and long, narrow shelves that strikingly store and display glassware. I have a friend in Brittany with a pine-paneled kitchen and no enclosed storage at all. Everything is placed on open shelves. "I find kitchen equipment very beautiful," she says, "and I like to see it all around me." In the French country kitchen, display's the thing.

SMALL BUT FULL OF SOUL

THE KITCHENS OF THREE STYLISH and supremely self-confident women highlight this section. Édith in Paris, Nathalie in the Île-de-France, and Isabelle in Provence are distinct personalities with very different homes and design sensibilities. What they have in common are very small kitchens that needed renovation and decoration. Édith's is in a turn-of-the-century Paris apartment in the 16th arrondissement; Nathalie's is in a quaint nineteenth-century village house; and Isabelle's is in a former grain mill surrounded by gardens near Lourmarin. With limited space, clever design and a refined sense of color are key. These three tiny, personal kitchens are little worlds that perfectly evoke their creators. 🐿

COUNTRY CHARM IN THE HEART OF PARIS

🐓

I'S A SMALL KITCHEN in a classic early-twentieth-century Paris apartment, overlooking a small garden in the affluent 16th arrondissement. What makes this kitchen soar above the mundane, and fills it with an enchanting spirit of country, is the beautifully conceived banquette dining corner, as well as the room's gentle vintage palette of cream, dove gray, and deep ruby red. "I wanted to have a very pretty table, flooded with natural light," says owner Édith de Ménibus. "My dream was to have a place where we could entertain elegantly, with the *esprit* of a dining room, yet still be in the kitchen."

Édith designed her kitchen around the dining area, a tiny world unto itself. Handsome cushions upholstered in a red-and-white check by Manuel

Canovas are suspended from a bistro-style brass railing, and matching banquette seating completes the confines of the L-shaped nook. Swedish Gustavian-style chairs by IKEA, refinished with a soft grayed patina, were upholstered in a red-grid Canovas fabric. Swathing the French windows, carnation-sprigged striped curtains, in a fabric by J. H. Thorp, pick up the red and gray colors in the dining area and add a merry country note. The dining area's greatest distinction—and strongest focal point—is the unusual collection of nineteenth-century art depicting domestic workers in grand homes.

Opposite Édith de Ménibus's romantic vintage palette of gray, cream, and ruby red suffuses her small apartment kitchen in Paris with country charm. Silver, crystal, art, and Édith's favorite red peonies set the stage at the cozy banquette table (*left*).

Above, left A collection of nineteenth-century art featuring domestic workers highlights the dining corner. Red-checked fabric by Manuel Canovas upholsters the banquette cushions. *Above, right* Beyond a whimsical ceramic hen pitcher, the refrigerator remains out of sight behind built-in cabinet doors.

In an "upstairs-downstairs" world, the subjects of these oil paintings and watercolors are players in the life "downstairs"—cooks, maids, butlers, delivery boys—and are painted with affection and humor. One painting reveals a parlor maid, duster in hand, stealing a kiss from a sculpted marble bust of a handsome aristocrat.

The vintage-looking kitchen floor, combining white glazed cement tiles accented by gray "dots," or *losanges,* is an important ele-

ment that ties the room harmoniously together. Countertops of charcoal-hued Italian
marble sit flush against a backsplash of ruby
red glazed ceramic tiles. Pale gray paneled
wood cabinets, designed by Édith, flank the
imposing SMEG six-burner range. Matching
cabinets near the entrance of the kitchen
hide the refrigerator, while the dishwasher
and a freezer are completely out of sight in a
back pantry. In this carefully edited kitchen,
functional appliances play a minor role.

A backsplash of ruby-glazed tiles set on the diagonal
above black marble countertops echoes the vivid red of
the floral print curtains from J. H. Thorp, as well as the
hues of the Canovas banquette cushions. Édith refinished
the Gustavian-style dining chairs from IKEA with a soft
grayed patina.

Soupe de Potiron

FRENCH PUMPKIN SOUP

Soupe de potiron, pumpkin soup, has been a fixture for more than a century at family tables in the French countryside, as well as at little country auberges from Normandy to Provence. Answering to several names in French—*potiron, citrouille, potimarron*—depending on its size and shape, the Gallic pumpkin is enjoying a long-overdue star turn in French cuisine. It can be found on the menus of top restaurants in hors d'oeuvres, appetizers, and brightly hued desserts. But pumpkin soup remains a classic, an easily prepared family favorite, as appropriate in a chic little kitchen in Paris as it is deep in the rural countryside. Be sure you buy a small pumpkin, such as a sugar pumpkin, suitable for cooking, not one that has been waxed or otherwise coated for display. Serve the pumpkin soup with grilled slices of baguette or country bread.

SERVES 6

4 cups chicken stock

1 (2$\frac{1}{2}$- to 3-pound) sugar pumpkin, peeled, seeded, and cut into small chunks

2 teaspoons sugar

Fine sea salt

1 tablespoon cornstarch

7 tablespoons unsalted butter, cut into bits

Freshly ground black pepper

$\frac{3}{4}$ cup crème fraîche

2 tablespoons chopped fresh chives

In a large casserole, bring the chicken stock to a boil over high heat. Add the pumpkin, sugar, and 1 teaspoon salt, and stir to combine. Return to a boil, cover, and reduce the heat to medium. Cook for about 18 minutes, until the pumpkin is tender. Remove the mixture from the heat and carefully transfer to a food processor. Process until thoroughly blended. Pour the mixture through a strainer back into the casserole, place over medium-high heat, and bring to a boil, stirring frequently, since the soup tends to scorch and stick to the bottom of the pot. Skim off any foam that forms on the top. Remove from the heat and set aside.

Combine the cornstarch with $\frac{1}{4}$ cup cold water and stir until it dissolves. Add to the pumpkin mixture and, using a large wooden spoon or a whisk, stir very well to blend. Return the casserole to medium-high heat and bring to a boil, stirring frequently. Add the butter and cook, still stirring frequently, until the mixture is smooth and unctuous, about 5 minutes. Season to taste with salt and pepper. Ladle into six soup bowls and top each serving with a dollop of crème fraîche, swirling it slightly. Sprinkle with the chives and serve immediately.

NATHALIE'S VINTAGE VILLAGE KITCHEN

NATHALIE BESNARD'S MOTHER, Martine Ouvrard, whose kitchen is featured on pages 20–27, always loved antiques and eventually made a profession out of her passion, opening Le Marquis de Carabas antiques shop in a village near Étampes. Nathalie has followed in her mother's stylish footsteps, opening an antiques and decorating shop next to her house in the posh little town of Soisy-sur-Seine, south of Paris. La Petite Fadette offers a combination of antique and contemporary items in an ambience of old-fashioned charm. The small kitchen of her nineteenth-century village home, which she shares with her husband and two daughters, reflects this same appealing mixture.

The kitchen occupies a small rectangular space at the back of the family's house. Stone steps lead from the kitchen to the backyard and the garden, giving the kitchen a more open feeling than if the two windows were the only apertures. The kitchen tiles are a blend of authentic antiques and vintage-style new. Hexagonal terra-cotta *tomettes*, for example, are salvaged nineteenth-century originals, while the rustic-looking white-glazed ceramic tiles on the countertop are new, produced by Josse, a company on the north coast of Brittany known for its beautiful vintage-style tiles. Above the antique oval stone sink is a faucet with sleek lines and a nostalgic look,

Opposite Antique elements and new materials with a vintage look, such as glazed tiles from Josse and cutwork cabinet trim, transform the once-mundane kitchen in Nathalie Besnard's nineteenth-century village home in the Île-de-France (*left*).

Above To detract from the massiveness of a large armoire in a small space, Nathalie replaced the doors' wood panels with chicken wire lined with beige linen. *Opposite* Below the antique oval stone sink, curtains that Nathalie stitched from checked fabric found in Sweden hide "unsightly things," she says.

purchased off the rack," says Nathalie, at the awesomely stocked Paris department store BHV, known especially for its great house-wares department. Nathalie's muted gray wall cabinets are both old *and* new, and very original. "The body of the cabinets is new," explains Nathalie, "from a suburban home center. I replaced the doors with a pair of old shutters I found at a salvage house. Then I designed and added the scalloped border along the bottom, to hide lights I installed under the cabinet."

Above, left At the far end of the kitchen, where a garden table with nineteenth-century chairs is set for two, an old radiator is unapologetically part of the décor. The still life painting with an eighteenth-century air is by Danielle Mercier. *Above, right* Nathalie showcases her flea-market collection of unframed, anonymous oil paintings ("Frames would take up too much space," says Nathalie) above the sofa in a sitting room just beyond the kitchen.

Nathalie kept her color palette neutral—gray, beige, and cream—accented with the pop of red in a carefully chosen checked fabric. "I love red," she says, "but not too much of it in a small kitchen. Here, it's perfect as an under-the-counter curtain softened by the neutrals. I looked a long time for a fabric with exactly this slightly muted shade of red. Finally, on a vacation in Sweden, I found it in a small shop and snapped it up." The curtains hide "unsightly things," says Nathalie, such as a garbage can, a small oven, and pantry items. Between the sink and the dining area, a marble-topped flea-market buffet serves as a room divider and an island.

The dominant piece of furniture in the kitchen is a large nineteenth-century armoire. Its volume in a small space pleases Nathalie, who replaced the wood panels of the doors with chicken wire, then lined the doors with beige linen. Two late-nineteenth-century wrought-iron garden chairs found in L'Isle-sur-la-Sorgue, the famous Provençal antiques center, flank a small round breakfast table. On the wall above the table hangs a distinct decorative link between mother Martine and daughter Nathalie: a small version of the eighteenth-century-inspired still life of fruits by Danielle Mercier that graces her mother's kitchen. It's a charming and affectionate note

Above, left Adding character and a nostalgic touch of the past, old shutters found at a salvage house replace the standard doors of "off-the-rack" cabinets from a home-supply center. *Above, right* A small guest bathroom off the kitchen repeats the red-and-white theme and skirted-sink motif of the kitchen.

Tarte aux Courgettes et au Basilic

ZUCCHINI AND BASIL TART

Nathalie loves cooking with fresh vegetables, often preparing tarts and casseroles with whatever is best from nearby markets. This simple, flavorful tart with a rich, flaky crust is good all year round, but especially in the summer when the zucchini and the basil come straight from local gardens. Serve it with a bright salad of bitter greens, such as arugula and watercress tossed with mesclun. Dress the salad just before serving with a light vinaigrette of olive oil, sherry vinegar, Dijon mustard, salt, and pepper.

SERVES 4 TO 6

For the pâte brisée à l'oeuf (flaky short-crust pastry)

1½ cups all-purpose flour

8 tablespoons (1 stick) unsalted butter, chilled and cut into small pieces

½ teaspoon fine sea salt

1 large egg, beaten

4 tablespoons ice water

For the filling

3 tablespoons extra-virgin olive oil

1 medium sweet onion, such as Vidalia, finely chopped

1¼ pounds zucchini (about 3 slim zucchini), sliced into ⅛-inch rounds

⅓ cup fresh basil, finely chopped

3 tablespoons heavy cream

1 teaspoon fine sea salt

½ teaspoon freshly ground black pepper

4 large eggs, beaten

TO MAKE THE PÂTE BRISÉE À L'OEUF: Combine the flour, butter, and salt in a food processor. Process for 10 to 12 seconds, until the mixture has a dry, crumbly texture resembling coarse cornmeal. Add the egg and the ice water to the mixture and pulse ten to twelve times, until the dough comes together in a smooth mass but before it forms into a ball. (The crust can become tough if processed even a few seconds too long.) If the dough seems too dry and dense, add 1 to 2 more tablespoons of ice water and pulse two or three times, or work in with your fingertips.

Remove the dough from the bowl and work it into a ball with your hands, then transfer it to a sheet of plastic wrap or wax paper. Flatten the dough into a neat, smooth disk, wrap, and refrigerate for at least 1 hour.

On a floured work surface, roll out the dough with a floured rolling pin into a large circle ⅛ inch thick and about 12 inches in diameter. Transfer the pastry circle to a buttered 9½-inch removable-bottom tart pan and press the dough gently into the bottom and fluted sides. Trim the dough so that just 1 inch extends above the rim. Fold this extension over upon itself to create a double-thick ¼-inch border above the rim. Flute the edges, prick the bottom of the pastry shell with a fork, cover with plastic wrap, and refrigerate for 15 minutes.

Preheat the oven to 375°F.

Line the tart shell with aluminum foil, then fill to the brim with dried beans, rice, or baking weights. Bake in the center of the oven for 8 minutes, remove the baking weights and the foil, then return to the oven and bake for 2 more minutes, so that the dough just dries a bit but does not color. Remove to a wire rack to cool. Maintain the oven temperature at 375°F.

TO MAKE THE FILLING: In a large skillet, heat the olive oil over medium-high heat. Add the onions and stir to coat with oil. Cook for 2 minutes, stirring frequently, then add the zucchini and stir until it is well coated with the oil. Reduce the heat to medium and cook the mixture until the onions and zucchini begin to turn translucent but not brown, about 3 minutes. Remove the skillet from the heat, transfer the mixture to a colander set over a plate, and drain off the liquid.

TO MAKE THE TART: Arrange the zucchini mixture in the baked crust, spreading it evenly over the bottom. Combine the basil, cream, salt, and pepper with the beaten eggs, and whisk to blend. Pour the egg mixture over the onion-and-zucchini mixture and bake the tart in the center of the oven for about 40 minutes, until the crust is a deep golden brown and the filling is firm and browned. Cool on a wire rack for 15 minutes. Serve warm, accompanied by a green salad.

(Photograph by Linda Dannenberg.)

The Chef's Wife Designs:
Isabelle's Kitchen

ÉDOUARD LOUBET made history in 1996 as the Michelin Guide's youngest starred chef, receiving his first star for the colorful, dazzling, and imaginative cuisine he created at the Moulin de Lourmarin in the Luberon region of Provence. There is never a trace of cream or butter in his cuisine, which emphasizes dishes made with olive and other oils. Today he cooks primarily at his second property, the Bastide de Capelongue, high on a hill in the village of Bonnieux. Many of the herbs and vegetables that inspire his cuisine come from the vast gardens on his estate near Lourmarin, where the fruits and vegetables grow among a heady assortment of more than 120 aromatic plants and herbs—lavender, rue, summer savory, families of basil, thyme, rosemary, parsley.

While the kitchens of the Moulin de Lourmarin and the Bastide de Capelongue are Édouard's domain, Édouard's willowy blond wife, Isabelle, insisted the kitchen at home be hers. "I wanted a simple, colorful family kitchen full of light, with everything arranged to my liking and my needs. Édouard has his professional kitchens at the restaurants, but this one is mine!"

The house, Isabelle explains, was originally a grain mill built in the 1800s with no kitchen facilities at all. "We wanted an ambience of 'Provençal country,'" says Isabelle.

Opposite An ensemble of regional elements, among them glazed tiles from Vernin Carreaux D'Apt and wrought ironwork from an atelier in Avignon, creates a vibrant kitchen composition at the Lourmarin home of chef Édouard Loubet and his wife, Isabelle. *Left* Édouard cooks with his son, Joseph, a budding chef.

Above, left Isabelle and Édouard always create family meals around the freshest local ingredients, such as Cavaillon melon for a first course, and green beans, tomatoes, and potatoes to accompany a roast chicken. *Above, right* A glass-fronted cabinet shelters Isabelle's collection of regional pottery.

"Very luminous, almost like a veranda with lots of glass opening onto a terrace." The Loubets opened up a small back room and stretched it out, in effect making it an extension of their terrace. One entire wall is glass and wrought iron, with sliding doors that open onto the terrace, giving the kitchen an airy, open feeling even though the space is actually quite small. The outside extends in, and vice versa. "We can enjoy the light, the sky, and the views across the terrace under the big mulberry tree," says Isabelle.

Édouard is a big booster of the local artisans, hiring them to do the iron, masonry, woodwork, and tile work at both the Moulin de Lourmarin and the Bastide de Capelongue. When it came to redoing the family

kitchen, he knew just whom to call. "All the ironwork in the kitchen—the iron facing for the refrigerator, the dishwasher, the garbage bin, and the doors of the cabinet under the sink—were done by Serge Baradian, one of the best *ferronniers* in Avignon." The iron facings cover the mundane façades of the appliances, and the cabinets were designed to match, giving a cohesive and original look to this small kitchen.

Other elements of the kitchen are also distinctly local. The oval dining table, which doubles as a work island, is crafted from *pierre de Cassis,* a dense, peach-hued limestone (it was used as the base for the Statue of Liberty) quarried near the seaside fishing village of Cassis. The old-fashioned French

A glass and wrought-iron wall with doors opening onto the terrace floods the kitchen with daylight and imparts the illusion of spaciousness to the small quarters. An iron-framed window high in the wall above the tiled backsplash opens the kitchen to morning light from the northeast.

stove is by Godin, with both electric and gas burners. The pale terra-cotta floor tiles are from L'Atelier de la Terre Cuite in Célony. And the dazzling, colorful backsplash and countertops of hand-cut, hand-glazed tiles are from the venerable Luberon firm Vernin Carreaux d'Apt, in Bonnieux.

Here in this happy, colorful domain the family cooks together. Perhaps the most enthusiastic participant is little Joseph, four, who loves to be sous-chef to Maman or Papa, adding bits of herb garnish, stirring the pot, grinding on a touch of black pepper, and running out to the vegetable garden to gather a handful of basil, a sprig of rosemary, or perhaps a warm, ripe tomato.

Left The chunky stone sink next to the Godin range has a deep basin side for washing dishes and a shallow basin for rinsing vegetables. Cabinet doors below are faced with wrought iron to match the dishwasher, the refrigerator, and the garbage bin. *Above* The Loubets—Isabelle and Édouard, with Joseph and Victoria—gather in the kitchen before lunch.

Poulet Rôti aux Herbes; Confit d'Ail

ROAST CHICKEN PROVENÇAL
WITH GARLIC CONFIT

This is a simple, classic roast chicken, savory with herbs, and accompanied by a meltingly tender and mild confit of garlic. Isabelle and Édouard serve it with vegetables such as sautéed French green beans, pan-grilled tomatoes, roasted or mashed potatoes, and a green salad. A small crock of the garlic confit in olive oil is offered on the side so that each diner can spread a clove or two on lightly toasted country bread.

SERVES 4 TO 6

For the garlic confit
1 head of garlic, divided into individual cloves, unpeeled
½ cup extra-virgin olive oil
2 fresh rosemary sprigs

For the roast chicken
One 3½- to 4-pound chicken
Fine sea salt
Freshly ground black pepper
Handful of fresh thyme sprigs
3 tablespoons unsalted butter
3 tablespoons extra-virgin olive oil
8 garlic cloves, unpeeled
½ cup chicken broth
¼ cup dry white vermouth

TO MAKE THE GARLIC CONFIT: In a small saucepan, combine the garlic, olive oil, and rosemary. Cook over low heat, stirring occasionally, until the garlic cloves are soft and tender when pressed with the tip of a small knife and the skin of the garlic begins to separate from the clove, about 40 minutes. The garlic should just heat gently rather than cook; never let it brown. Remove the garlic confit from heat, and set aside in the pan to cool. The confit can be stored in the refrigerator in a tightly sealed glass jar for one week. Serve at room temperature in a small ceramic crock or bowl.

TO MAKE THE CHICKEN: Preheat the oven to 375°F.

Season the cavity of the chicken with salt and pepper, and stuff with the fresh thyme. Truss the legs. In a copper or stainless-steel roasting pan that can cook on the stovetop, melt the butter over medium heat. Turn the heat up to medium-high, place the chicken in the pan, and turn it over several times in the pan to coat with the butter. Brown the chicken evenly on all sides, just until it takes on a nice golden color, 8 to 10 minutes. Remove from the heat and carefully pour out all the butter in the pan. (It might be easier to do this if you transfer the chicken to a plate momentarily, then return it to the pan.) Discard the butter. Drizzle the olive oil over the chicken and season with salt and pepper. Scatter the 8 garlic cloves around the chicken. Roast in the center of the oven for about 1 hour and 15 minutes, until the chicken is a deep golden brown and the juices run clear when the thigh is pierced gently with the tip of a sharp knife. Remove from the oven and transfer the chicken to a platter.

Meanwhile, using a slotted spoon, remove the garlic cloves from the roasting pan and set aside. Place the pan over medium-high heat and bring the pan drippings to a boil. Add the chicken broth and the vermouth. Then, using a wooden spoon or a spatula, deglaze the pan, scraping up the brown bits and stirring constantly, until the sauce thickens slightly, 5 to 7 minutes. Remove from the heat, spoon off any fat floating on the top of the sauce, then transfer the mixture to a warmed sauceboat, first pouring it through a mesh strainer. Carve the chicken and arrange on the platter with the reserved roasted garlic cloves. Serve immediately with the sauce and garlic confit.

KITCHEN ARTS AND COLLECTIBLES

WHAT YOU DISPLAY IN YOUR KITCHEN CAN BE AS IMPORTANT AS THE TILES YOU CHOOSE FOR THE BACKSPLASH, YOUR FLOOR PATTERN, AND YOUR CABINETS. IT WAS A LONG TIME AGO, DURING AN EARLY TRIP TO FRANCE AFTER COLLEGE, BUT I'LL NEVER FORGET THE FIRST time I saw an eighteenth-century oil painting over a kitchen sink, right above the faucets. The kitchen, I thought, was for decorating with more whimsical, less valuable art: some vintage publicity posters, perhaps, a set of flea-market plates, or some framed botanical prints of herbs. But an eighteenth-century oil painting just inches above the faucets, within splash range? Many years and many visits to French homes later, I am no longer surprised to find real art in the kitchen. As one home owner told me, "I love to cook and I spend hours of time every week in the kitchen. It's where friends gather to have a glass of wine and chop a few carrots while I prepare the dinner. Why not be surrounded by paintings you love in the kitchen?"

A large kitchen with generous wall space invites display. When an acquaintance was roughing out the design of her new kitchen in Provence, to be converted from a *grange* attached to the house, the first thing she thought of—even before she had chosen the massive stove that reigns in the kitchen—was a wall-sized painting she had recently purchased at a local gallery. "I made sure," she says, "that there would be enough wall space to accommodate that painting."

Not only large kitchens are suitable places for oil paintings and watercolors. A handsomely framed painting or a collection of nineteenth-century watercolors lends importance to a small kitchen as well. Two small kitchens in Paris that I find particularly beguiling both have valuable art on view. In one, a nineteenth-century still life with game in an ornate gilt frame hangs, like the very first kitchen oil painting I saw, within a foot of the vintage brass faucet and the sink. It is appreciated frequently throughout the day, and the occasional spritz of water is simply patted away with a towel. In the other kitchen, a collection of fifteen winsome nineteenth-century watercolors of domestic life hangs above the dining table, forming the room's striking centerpiece. Antique botanical prints have been wildly popular in home decoration for years. In the south of France, this longtime trend is more recherché; antique botanicals, with the actual ancient herb or flower pressed onto a page and identified in antique script, are the ne plus ultra in this domain, highly sought after in antiques shops and flea markets. A kitchen I visited near Fontaine-de-Vaucluse was embellished with a rare collection of these antique botanical pressings, in two rows of four stretching along the countertop. The collection is what the eye first sees on entering the room, and it is what I remember most vividly.

In the apartment kitchen of celebrated Paris chef Michel Rostang, an inveterate collector who haunts the Paris flea markets, a lavishly gilt-framed still life of fresh game hangs within inches of a graceful vintage brass faucet.

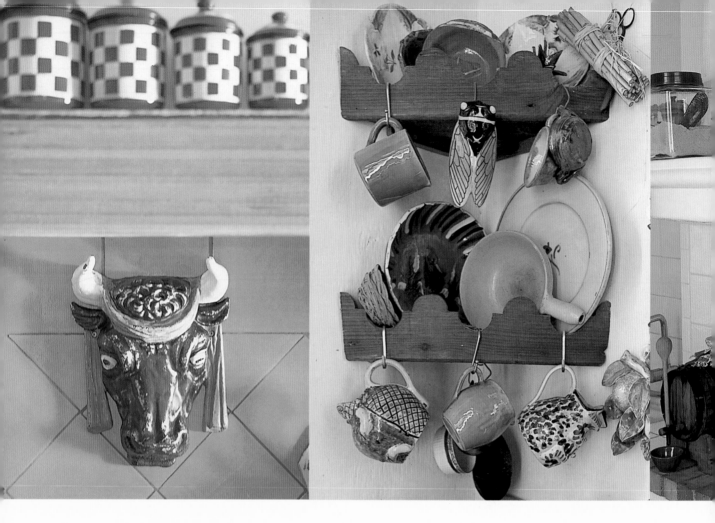

Clockwise from above left A ribbon-swagged Provençal bull's head from a 1930s butcher shop keeps decorator Nono Girard company in her Carpentras kitchen; at the Mas de Barbut, Provençal and Mexican pottery deck two corner kitchen shelves; flea-market collectibles, including a market sign for chives, pick up the blue-and-white theme of Patricia Wells's Paris kitchen; Philippe Irrmann's culinary collection includes a set of handmade eighteenth-century graters, and glazed eighteenth-century ocher and brown crockery (*below, right*); antique copperware catches the sun in the Camargue kitchen of the Mas de Peint; an early-twentieth-century clock from the Reveillon chocolate company keeps the family on time in the Paris kitchen of chef Michel Rostang; a collection of whimsical early-twentieth-century salt and pepper shakers produced as promotional items by the Lustucru pasta company gathers on a cutting board in Paris.

Almost every kitchen I visited, whether it was sleekly contemporary or rustic and old-fashioned, displayed some form of vintage collectible: *true* vintage—that is, not distressed reproductions. Authenticity is key. The kitchen seems to awaken a sense of nostalgia in so many people, perhaps because it is a room that evokes happy memories of childhood with a parent or a grandparent at the stove, and joyful family meals. Or else it inspires thoughts of what family life in a kitchen should have been, could have been, and can still be in a kitchen of one's own. Collectibles in a kitchen often reflect a personal passion. Food writer Patricia Wells has a passion for Paris, as well as a love for all things culinary, and the petite kitchen of her Left Bank Paris apartment, with its vintage saltshakers, market signs,

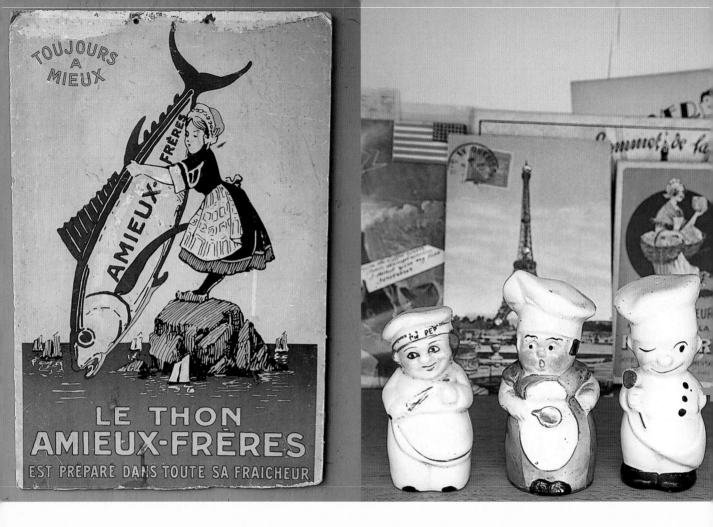

Clockwise from above left A 1930s period poster from Brittany advertises "the best" canned tuna; a trio of vintage saltshakers stands out on a shelf of collectibles in the Paris kitchen of food writer Patricia Wells; a 1980s oil painting by Provençal painter Gérard Drouillet draws the eye above a nineteenth-century *sécretaire,* or drop-leaf desk, in Michel Biehn's Provençal kitchen; a collection of melon-related *objets* crowds the *bibliothèque* shelves of melon-loving chef Jean-Jacques Prévot in Cavaillon; Philippe Irrmann's extraordinary collection of eighteenth-century culinary *objets* includes a selection of elegant copper molds.

and postcards, reflects both of these themes. A passion for Paris is also evident on the shelves of a restored Burgundy farmhouse kitchen I know, where Eiffel Tower memorabilia adorns the shelves.

In some kitchens, the collectibles reflect a love for a specialized kind of object. Acclaimed Paris chef Michel Rostang is fascinated by vintage advertising memorabilia, as his Paris apartment kitchen attests. In the Camargue region of Provence, the owners of the sun-washed Mas de Peint Hotel treasure a collection of antique wooden salt and flour boxes—*salières* and *farinières*—which they display on the marble countertops in the kitchen. Moving west into Languedoc, Danielle and Jean-Claude Gandon, the proprietors of the Mas de Barbut, an atmospheric bed-and-breakfast (see pages 139–45), are smitten

with all kinds of pottery—mugs, pitchers, platters, and bowls—from France and Mexico.

A kitchen's art and *objets* might also mirror an owner's love for a particular period of time, as in the kitchen of chef Carole Peck and her husband, Bernard Jarrier, in the Provençal village of Montfrin. Bernard and Carole love all things art deco, and it shows—not only in Carole's extraordinary jewelry, but in the posters, paintings, furniture, and collectibles that embellish the room (among them a dazzling yellow-and-blue poster from the early 1930s advertising canned tuna from Brittany, and jewel-bright green-and-white art deco lamps from the 1920s). The art and collectibles in a kitchen personalize it like nothing else can, revealing hints of lives and loves, and creating a room that tells a story.

CONTEMPORARY COUNTRY

*C*ONTEMPORARY IS A WORD that connotes the spirit of today, the vibe of our time, a freshness of perception. In design, it can mean spare, functional architecture or furnishings in state-of-the-art materials such as brushed steel, solar glass panels, and ceramic fibers. But contemporary isn't limited to the modern. It can mean a novel look at the traditional, or a new approach to the classics. The four kitchens in the following pages portray fresh visions of French country—contemporary, but with a reverence for the past. A village kitchen west of the Rhône is modern in feeling but embellished with wonderful art deco collectibles. In the isolated *mas* near Saint-Rémy-de-Provence, the kitchen and dining room reflect the owners' love of Asia. An art collection inspired an airy farmhouse kitchen in the Luberon. And in Clermont-Ferrand, a clever architect put most of his kitchen on wheels. In the best of French design, yesterday always informs today. 🐾

Zen Tranquillity in the Heart of Provence

A T THE END of a sun-baked, rocky dirt road, with nary a signpost to be seen, lies this enchanting *mas*. The house was a crumbling wreck with bad plumbing, but the setting and the unparalleled views of the Alpilles, the Alpine foothills that separate the region of Les Baux from that of Saint-Rémy, seduced the owners. The house was gutted and renovated with the talents and vision of local Saint-Rémy architect Hugues Bosc. Today the property boasts a rose-bordered swimming pool and, high on a hill facing west, a cottage-like gazebo for enjoying cocktails and gazing at the sunset on a hot summer's eve.

The house, purely Provençal in mood, design, and materials, offers up space to a significant collection of Asian art gathered during years of

work and travel through Japan, Singapore, Cambodia, and China. The juxtaposition of the local terra-cotta tile flooring, gray marble-like countertops quarried in the northern Rhône Valley, and buffed-blue artisanal cabinets with the Asian accents is striking but completely harmonious. In fact, a certain Zen tranquillity and order pervades the household.

The dramatic kitchen, bold in color and scale, opens onto the large dining area with a table that seats fourteen. "We wanted a kitchen that was part of the dining room, one that flowed into the dining space gracefully,"

Opposite A seventeenth-century Italian refectory table, with a quartet of seventeenth-century Japanese temple candelabra posed like sentinels on each corner, leads into the open kitchen of an isolated, tree-shaded *mas* near Saint-Rémy-de-Provence (*left*).

The elegant form of the white-trimmed fireplace mantel is repeated in the cooking alcove to conceal over-the-cooktop lighting and ventilation. The floor lamp was converted from an imposing candleholder created for an English castle.

the home owners say. "And we wanted a kitchen that was beautiful, but not too 'kitcheny,' with strong, elegant lines and beautiful materials." The kitchen harmonizes with the dramatic presence of the owners' beloved antique art and collectibles in the dining room—such as a large, graphic collage of antique porcelain Chinese heads and the bold wooden floor lamps converted by the owners from candleholders created for the halls of an English castle.

"I didn't want a kitchen overwhelmed with

appliances," notes the wife. "I wanted a discreet cooking and preparation area, without a huge flashy stove or any large, hot ovens. It just gets too hot in the summer, when we spend most of our time here." Preparations for entertaining are smoothly accomplished, and with a minimum of fuss, with a two-burner glass cooktop, a large gas burner next to it, and a small wall oven. When the owners entertain, they often invite a crowd, from eight to twenty people, but menus are kept simple with dinners featuring casseroles, roasts, and salads.

Three burners, one gas and two electric, suffice in this pared-down kitchen, where the owner's generations-old collection of antique copperware and brass gleams above the gray *pierre de Tavel* stone countertops.

Two elements of the kitchen contribute to its dynamic style. One is the eye-catching hand-buffed shade of deep blue, somewhere between French and Prussian in hue, that enrobes the cupboards and cabinets. The color reflects the tones of a collection of antique blue enamelware pots and pitchers above the cupboard, acquired over several visits to the antiques mecca L'Isle-sur-la-Sorgue. A grouping of gleaming eighteenth and nineteenth-century copperware, all family heirlooms from the wife's mother, is the second element that embellishes this kitchen, catching light from both north- and south-facing windows and bathing the cooktop in the reflected glow.

Opposite Custom cabinets with brass pulls are finished with a lime-based paint in an unusual patinated blue inspired by the owners' collection of vintage blue enamelware pitchers and pots. *Above, left* The morning sun silhouettes two sculptural blown-glass oil and vinegar cruets on the windowsill. *Above, right* The built-in cabinets include shelves for favorite cookbooks and a pair of cabinets with wire-mesh-covered diamond cutouts in the doors for visual interest and aerated storage. The tall blue cabinet beyond the sink camouflages the dishwasher.

Tian d'Agneau

PROVENÇAL LAMB CASSEROLE WITH EGGPLANT, CUCUMBER, AND RICE

This hearty one-pot meal, a savory Provençal lamb stew with rice and vegetables, is a perfect fall or winter dish. Serve it with crusty bread, a green salad, and a full-bodied Côte-du-Rhône such as a Gigondas.

SERVES 6 TO 8

7 tablespoons extra-virgin olive oil, plus additional as needed

2 medium onions, sliced

4 garlic cloves, crushed

3 pounds boneless lamb shoulder, cut into 1½-inch cubes

1 tablespoon chopped fresh thyme leaves

1 tablespoon chopped fresh rosemary

Fine sea salt

Freshly ground black pepper

2 long, firm medium eggplants (about 1 pound each), sliced into ⅓-inch rounds

3 cups cooked long-grain rice (about ¾ cup uncooked)

2 tablespoons tomato paste

1 cup beef broth or water

4 bay leaves, plus more for garnish

2 medium zucchini, sliced into ⅓-inch rounds

1 hothouse (seedless) cucumber, sliced into ⅓-inch rounds

3 tablespoons chopped fresh flat-leaf parsley

In a large skillet, heat 4 tablespoons of the olive oil over medium heat. Add the onions and garlic and sauté, stirring frequently, just until the onions are translucent but not browned, 4 to 5 minutes. (Do not let the garlic brown; if the cloves begin to take on color, remove them from the pan immediately and set aside in a separate bowl to await the onions.) Using a slotted spatula, remove the mixture to a bowl and set aside.

Add another tablespoon of olive oil to the skillet, raise the heat to medium-high, then add the lamb, thyme, and rosemary and stir to combine. Brown the lamb evenly on all sides, about 6 minutes. Return the onions to the skillet (and the garlic if you've set the cloves aside), stir to incorporate with the lamb, then remove the mixture from the heat. Season with salt and pepper, then transfer the lamb mixture to a large bowl and set aside.

Return the skillet to medium-high heat, add 2 tablespoons of the olive oil, and heat. Brown the eggplant slices in batches, evenly on both sides, about 2 minutes per side. Add 1 tablespoon of olive oil to the skillet before each new batch. Transfer to a plate, sprinkle with salt and pepper, and set aside.

Preheat the oven to 325°F.

Add the rice and the tomato paste to the lamb mixture and stir to thoroughly combine. Spoon half of the lamb and rice mixture into the bottom of a Dutch oven or other heavy-bottomed large casserole. Pour ½ cup of the beef broth over the lamb mixture, and top with 2 bay leaves. Layer the zucchini slices over the lamb mixture, followed by the cucumber slices and the browned eggplant slices. Season with salt and pepper. Spoon in the remaining lamb and rice mixture, pour in the remaining ½ cup of beef broth, and top with 2 bay leaves.

Place a sheet of aluminum foil over the top of the casserole, shiny side up, then cover with the lid. Bake in the center of the oven for 2 hours, until the lamb is tender. Check once or twice during the cooking time to make sure the mixture isn't getting too dry. If the mixture is sticking to the sides of the casserole, add ¼ to ½ cup of water. Remove from the oven, garnish with chopped parsley and a few bay leaves, and serve.

A Connecticut Yankee
Cooks in Montfrin

LE PRIEURÉ NOTRE-DAME, the family home of chef Carole Peck and her French publisher husband, Bernard Jarrier, is tucked into a tiny street across from a sixteenth-century stone church in the sleepy Provençal village of Montfrin. The house was the church's former priory, with architectural roots dating back to the twelfth century. Within the confines of its solid old bones, the antique house has a décor inspired by the couple's passion for art deco, art moderne, and the quirky *objet*. Vintage treasures from the nineteenth to mid-twentieth centuries embellish almost every surface, from the sunburst metal mirror that tops the fifteenth-century fireplace to lounge chairs in the salon from the great French steamship the *Île-de-France.* "Style is like

food," says Bernard. "In the best design, as in the best meals, there is *un fil conducteur*, a unifying theme."

Carole's long, beamed kitchen, opening onto a small courtyard swimming pool, exemplifies this theme with period furniture and accessories, while at the same time offering professional-level practicality. "My dream was to create a kitchen that combined utility and whimsy," says Carole, the renowned chef of the Good News Café in Woodbury, Connecticut. "We wanted a very workable kitchen filled with the objects and furniture that we've fallen in love with over the years in markets

Opposite In the large, beamed kitchen of chef Carole Peck's antique village home in Montfrin, just west of Avignon across the Rhône (*left*), a 1920s baker's rack holds her prized collection of vintage copperware.

throughout France. We have decorative vintage elements, such as paintings and a 1920s advertising poster for canned tuna fish, and very useful old items as well, such as the two-inch-thick marble slabs on the countertop that came from an old pâtisserie. The new elements that we added, such as the backsplash of tumbled marble, we kept neutral and discreet. For flooring, we chose a stone-gray, rubber-lined, natural fiber industrial carpeting instead of tile. It's a surface that's easier on your back when you're cooking than cement or terra-cotta tiles."

At one end of the kitchen, near the sliding doors to the courtyard, a suite of 1940s walnut chairs surrounds a hand-hammered copper table with wrought-iron legs, a prototype from Morocco. A vintage 1920s baker's rack near the stove holds antique copper, while two green-and-white art deco lamps shine softly on an inlaid oak-and-ceramic buffet from the 1940s. Along one wall is a rolling garage-mechanic's rack from the 1930s, found in a shop in L'Isle-sur-la-Sorgue, the Provençal antiques paradise. Carole and Bernard have left original traces of mechanic's oil on the bottom for the sake of *nostalgie*.

The heart of this kitchen, however, has nothing to do with vintage and everything to

The dining area, with an unusual 1940s oak buffet inset with ceramic panels and a wrought-iron and copper table, leads into Carole's kitchen, where a wide swath of tumbled marble forms the backsplash. Collectible bowls, which she loves, line an antique beam over the cooking alcoves that shelter three Viking ranges—two traditional models, and a Chinese stove with an inset wok. For her kitchen floor, Carole opted for stone-colored natural-fiber industrial carpeting rather than traditional tiles.

Above, left A suite of 1940s French walnut chairs surrounds the Moroccan hand-hammered copper dining table with wrought-iron legs in the dining area. *Above, right* Above an art deco pedestal table in the salon just beyond the kitchen, a young girl gazes out from an early 1950s portrait painted in Lyon. *Opposite, left* A rolling mechanic's rack from the 1930s is reborn as a showcase for Carole and Bernard's colorful collection of Vallauris pottery. *Opposite, right* Carole slices and dices at her custom-designed granite-topped center island.

do with efficiency, practicality, and the joy of cooking. Dominating the center of the room is an enormous island composed of an *enfilade* of low professional pastry coolers topped by a huge slab of granite. The kitchen was designed for a convivial crowd of dicers, choppers, mincers, peelers, and kibitzers, and for a very specific reason. Four or five times a year during their stints in Provence, Carole and Bernard host a popular weeklong culinary tour of Provence for small groups of dedicated foodies. The program is a mix of cooking classes with Carole and other celebrated local chefs, shopping in local markets, wine and olive oil tastings,

and eating at the region's best restaurants and bistros. The kitchen is base camp for the tour and is the setting for some of the week's happiest moments. Around the island, eight to ten people work comfortably preparing recipes, all the while sipping chilled rosé and nibbling olives. Carole's kitchen, like every great kitchen, invites intimacy and camaraderie.

Out of this kitchen come Carol's heavenly and homey Provençal dishes, such as caviar d'aubergines, an eggplant caviar; tapenade, a paste of green or black olives; aigo boulido, the classic Provençal garlic soup said to cure everything from a hangover to the flu;

roasted quail stuffed with thyme, paired with honey-roasted pears; baked swiss chard with fennel; poached figs in sweet bandol wine; and clafouti with mirabelle plums. Lunch, such as a *salade composée* with potatoes, artichokes, eggs, and green beans, is often served on the terrace by the pool, to serve and clear, while dinners are enjoyed in the stone-walled *cave,* a cozy niche discovered under the ancient spiral stone stairway. With the tables dressed in vintage linens and set with antique crystal, porcelain, and faience, dinners in the *cave*, with candlelight playing off the sixteenth-century stonework, are a feast for all the senses.

Cailles au Thym, avec des Poires Rôties et Chou Sauté

ROAST QUAILS WITH HONEY-ROASTED PEARS AND WILTED SAVOY CABBAGE

When Carole prepares this dish at her home in Montfrin, she walks out the door to the local *boucherie* to purchase her fresh quails, then crosses the little road to the grocer for her pears and thyme. She has all kinds of honey on hand—some perfumed with lavender, some with rosemary blossoms, some with chestnut blossoms—but any aromatic honey will work well. French quails are larger than their American counterparts, so here you will need two quails per person. You could also substitute squab, poussin chicken, or cornish hens, in which case one per diner will suffice. Prepare the cabbage while the quails and pears are roasting.

SERVES 4

For the quails
8 whole quails, bone in
Leaves from 16 thyme sprigs
2 tablespoons fine sea salt
2 teaspoons coarsely ground black pepper
8 large garlic cloves, peeled and smashed
¼ cup vegetable oil

For the honey-roasted pears
4 tablespoons (½ stick) unsalted butter, cut into 4 pieces
2 large pears, Bosc or Bartlett, peeled, halved, and cored
Juice of 1 lemon
½ cup fragrant honey

TO PREPARE THE QUAILS: Preheat the oven to 400°F.

Clean the birds' cavities and tuck the wings under their backs.

Season the inside of each quail with the thyme, salt, and pepper. Place a clove of garlic in each quail (use 2 cloves each if using larger birds). Next, use cotton twine to truss the legs together. Wrap the twine around the quails, making a knot at the neck bone. Set aside in the refrigerator while you prepare the pears.

TO MAKE THE PEARS: In a ceramic or enamel baking dish, place the butter pieces with one pear half on top of each, core sides facing down. Squeeze the lemon juice over the pears. Drizzle a spoonful of honey over each pear. Place in the same preheated oven as the quails, next to them, or on the rack below, and cook until tender, approximately 15 minutes. Remove, cover loosely with aluminum foil, and set aside.

TO ASSEMBLE THE DISH: When you are ready to roast the birds, place a metal roasting pan in the oven to preheat, 6 to 7 minutes. Rub the birds with the oil, then place the quails breast side up in the hot roasting pan. Roast for about 20 minutes, until golden brown. (*Note:* roast squabs and poussin for about 30 minutes; cornish hens, for about 35 minutes.) Remove from the oven. Discard the twine and serve the quails alongside the pears on a platter lined with raw cabbage leaves, spooning on any extra pan drippings from the quails and the pears. Serve accompanied by a platter of Wilted Savoy Cabbage.

Wilted Savoy Cabbage

1 small head Savoy cabbage

¼ cup extra-virgin olive oil

3 shallots, finely diced

2 tablespoons Dijon mustard

Fine sea salt

Freshly ground black pepper

Remove the outer large green leaves of the cabbage. (You may wash these and set aside to present your completed dinner on if you like.) Quarter the cabbage and cut out the core. Shred the cabbage into ¼-inch slices. Heat the olive oil in a sauté pan. Add the shallots and cook briefly to soften, about a minute or so. Add the cabbage and cook until wilted, stirring occasionally, about 10 minutes. When the cabbage is wilted, add the mustard and salt and pepper; stir to incorporate. Serve immediately.

Cooking and Canvases: The Artful Kitchen

TANDRA FELL IN LOVE with her classic eighteenth-century Provençal *mas*, or farmhouse, more than twenty years ago, when the space now occupied by her kitchen still had a dirt floor. Directly attached to the main part of the house, the kitchen area was once the barn, and surprisingly had remained so until almost the end of the twentieth century. The house needed a total renovation and modernization—it was a real fixer-upper—but Tandra was smitten with its history, its stone-paved lavender garden, its views over neighboring vineyards, and its potential. "To me the house was like a beautiful lady gone to ruin," she says. "I wanted to bring her back. I walked through the house and saw the great bones of the original construction—the volumes,

the beams, the apertures, and the fabulous wall space. In the dark barn, I could imagine a kitchen, full of light and hung with some of my favorite art."

The first order of business in the transformation was removing the tall, gently arched barn doors and replacing them with wrought-iron-framed French doors topped by a contemporary, Palladian-style window, the kitchen's one source of natural light. Then came the choice of flooring. "I didn't want to lay a new stone or tile floor that would abut and conflict with the eighteenth-century stone floors of the living

Opposite "The Sky Is the Limit" exclaims the joyful triptych painting by California artist Carole Akins that is the centerpiece of an art-oriented kitchen in a restored Luberon *mas* with a lavender-filled garden (*left*) and panoramic views.

Above Working at her limestone sink, Tandra can gaze upon a bucolic eighteenth-century landscape painting with the iconic Pont du Gard bridge in the background. *Opposite* Lighted by an electrified eighteenth-century lantern, an immense nineteenth-century fabric-cutter's table provides all the workspace Tandra needs when preparing dinner for friends.

room," she says. "So I decided on something completely different—polished concrete that went through a special multilayering process to achieve its beautiful, subtle patina." Tandra then had the massive beams, as thick as tree trunks, plastered over and painted white. The walls were painted white as well, to show her paintings to best advantage.

All of the essential kitchen components—stove, sink, dishwasher, limestone-topped cabinets—were designed by a *cuisiniste*, a custom-kitchens firm called Mouvements, in Avignon, to line up against the 25-foot back wall. The La Cornue range is a commanding, custom-built black iron, stainless steel, and brass behemoth with the name of the house, Mas de la Calade, emblazoned on a brass plaque. The large sink, with its graceful, faintly Louis XV–style silhouette, was custom carved from golden-hued Provençal limestone. Nearby, a large nineteenth-century cherrywood chest-on-chest holds glassware and dishes. Running along the floor by the work area is a long, antique Oriental rug found on a foray to L'Isle-sur-la-Sorgue. "Everyone told me I was crazy to put an Oriental rug there," Tandra says, "but I love it. It adds color and divides the space."

Furniture in the kitchen is kept to a few well-chosen antiques, most, like the carpet, discovered in L'Isle-sur-la-Sorgue. The centerpiece of the room is an almost 10-foot-long, early-nineteenth-century cutter's table from a defunct local fabric company. The table functions as an enormous center island, with storage for large pots on a low shelf, and a generous work space for food prep—

with an antique marble pastry slab on one end and a thick butcher's block on the other. Guests gather at a simple walnut drop-leaf table surrounded by slipcovered wrought-iron chairs for dinners on chilly evenings, or outside on the terrace when the weather is balmy. Recessed lighting illuminates the work area above the stone sink and the oven, while electrified eighteenth-century wrought-iron lanterns found in a nearby antiques shop shine down on the dining area. A tall, steel-framed mirror, which Tandra added to break up a long stretch of bare wall, reflects the scene.

The paintings that Tandra envisioned when she first set eyes on the property now grace the walls. Over the sink, like a window into another world, is a late-eighteenth-century pastoral Provençal farm landscape with cows in the foreground and the old Roman bridge, the Pont du Gard, in the background. On the wall to the right of the front entrance is a glowing eighteenth-century French rendering of the Annunciation with the Virgin Mary and the archangel Gabriel. The pièce de résistance is a large contemporary painting by California artist Carole Akins. Vivid and joyous, the triptych tableau comprises the portraits of three women, with a legend floating above them like skywriting: "The Sky Is The Limit."

Light pouring through wrought-iron framed French doors casts a celestial glow on an eighteenth-century French painting of the Annunciation. Billowing glazed-cotton curtains in an eighteenth-century floral garland print from Pierre Frey's Comoglio collection elegantly accentuate the kitchen's dramatic proportions.

Tarte Tatin à la Tandra

TANDRA'S TARTE TATIN

This lushly delicious upside-down caramelized apple tart is said to have originated with two nineteenth-century sisters named Tatin who worked at their family hotel and restaurant in the Loire Valley town of Lamotte-Beuvron. There are many variations on the basic recipe of apples sautéed in butter and sugar and then baked with a crust on top and inverted before serving. This is Tandra's, a dessert that leaves her friends clamoring for more.

SERVES 6 TO 8

6 tablespoons unsalted butter

¹/₂ cup granulated sugar

6 large Golden Delicious apples, peeled, cored, and quartered

1 recipe Pâte Brisée (Sweetened Short-Crust Pastry), page 27

3 tablespoons turbinado natural cane raw sugar or Brownulated sugar (optional)

1 cup crème fraîche

In a 12-inch cast-iron skillet, melt the butter over medium heat. Sprinkle the granulated sugar over the bottom of the pan, stir to blend, and cook for 1 minute, until the sugar starts to dissolve. Remove the skillet from the heat. Tightly pack the apple slices in the skillet, arranging them in an overlapping circle around the outside edge of the skillet. Fill in the center of the skillet with apples, pushing in as many as possible so that no space remains between any slices.

Return the skillet to medium heat and cook, shaking the pan frequently, and occasionally nudging the slices very gently, to prevent burning on the bottom, until the sugar caramelizes—thickening and turning a deep golden brown color—about 30 minutes. Remove the pan from the heat and set aside.

Preheat the oven to 425°F.

On a floured work surface, roll out the dough with a floured rolling pin into a circle ¹/₈ inch thick and about 13 inches in diameter. When the skillet has cooled slightly, place the dough circle on top of the apples. Tuck the edges of the dough in around the apples. Bake in the center of the oven for 25 to 30 minutes, until the dough is deep golden brown. Transfer to a wire rack to cool slightly, about 15 minutes. Run a knife around the inside edge of the skillet to loosen the crust and apples. Place a heat-proof serving platter on top of the skillet, and, wearing oven mitts, invert the tart onto the platter, apple side up. Return any apples sticking to the skillet to their proper position on top of the tart. If you wish, sprinkle the tart with turbinado or Brownulated sugar. Serve lukewarm with a spoonful of crème fraîche on the side. You can make the tart up to eight hours ahead of time and let it stand at room temperature. Reheat the tart to lukewarm in a warm oven before serving.

MEALS ON WHEELS: AN ARCHITECT'S OPEN KITCHEN

IN THIS STRIKINGLY imaginative kitchen, transformed along with the rest of the house from a 1950s commercial garage, almost nothing is set in stone—or in cement, plaster, or wood, for that matter. Everything, save for the large professional range, is on rubber wheels. This concept is certainly appropriate for a kitchen in the Auvergne town of Clermont-Ferrand, home to the Michelin Tire Company, but proximity to Michelin was not the designer's guiding purpose. "I wasn't sure anything would stay where I originally put it," says architect Bernard Murat of the design for his own kitchen. "I wanted the ultimate flexibility to reposition all the elements if necessary. Even the kitchen sink has wheels, and plastic tubing instead of metal pipes,

so it is mobile as well. So far, nothing has moved from where I originally placed it, but we always have the option."

The kitchen is wide open to the living room. "My wife, Véronique, and I absolutely didn't want separate spaces, with a kitchen closed off from the rest of the house," says Bernard. "I wanted to be able to stay in the kitchen while my friends were in the living room and be able to see them and be part of the conversation while I was cooking. I did install sliding glass panels between the spaces, but I don't think we've ever closed them."

Opposite Bernard Murat and his wife, Véronique, prepare dinner in their open redwood and steel Clermont-Ferrand kitchen, where almost everything is on wheels. The menu often calls for the fresh herbs (*left*), which flourish in an umbrella stand planter on the deck.

Beyond a movable island topped with a thick slab of Brazilian blue granite, the appliances line up under glass-paneled fluorescent lighting. The large professional-style Westahl range in the center is the only stationary element in the kitchen.

Two design elements dominate the décor—redwood and stainless steel, a pairing not commonly seen. The floors are redwood, as are the cabinet doors and drawers. Redwood floor-to-ceiling cabinets cover one wall. Stainless steel frames the cabinets and forms the backsplash across the work area. "Stainless steel and redwood are two elements I find very beautiful," Bernard says.

The kitchen equipment stretches across the back wall, dominated in the center by a large, professional-style Westahl range, a modern line by the venerable Lacanche appliance company. A glass-and-metal *marquis*, or panel, conceals both the fluorescent lighting and the stove's ventilation system. Large,

square terra-cotta tiles in a warm earth tone cover the wall behind the kitchen *enfilade*.

Facing the sink is a large center island—on wheels, of course. A majestic slab of Brazilian blue granite covers one end of the island, and a butcher's block covers the other. Vintage elements such as bentwood bistro chairs from Bernard's grandparents' hotel, a 1950s wall-mounted glass mosaic advertising a strawberry liqueur, and a red-lacquered Chinese cabinet add color and character to the kitchen's sleek, contemporary décor.

Both of them enthusiastic cooks, Bernard and Véronique often invite friends to join them for dinner at the nineteenth-century

Bernard's passion for redwood is evident in the kitchen's redwood floors, redwood and steel island, and redwood floor-to-ceiling cabinets. Adding a striking jewel-red accent is a vintage glass mosaic on the wall above the sink advertising a strawberry liqueur.

Previous pages Vintage Oriental rugs, heirlooms from Bernard's grandparents, break up the sea of redwood flooring. *Above, left* A red-lacquered Chinese cabinet purchased at the flea market stores the many exotic spices Bernard and Véronique use in their cooking. Peeking out from the walls, glass pocket doors were designed to divide the kitchen and the living area, but, as Bernard confesses, "We've never used them." *Above, right* Dinner is served on the broad wood deck that overlooks the treetops and rooftops of Clermont-Ferrand.

extension table placed between the kitchen and the living area, or out on the broad wood deck, where two granite-topped tables—yes, mounted on wheels—can accommodate a crowd of fourteen. They prefer easy, savory grilled scallops with lime, or risotto with tomatoes and Parmesan, one of Bernard's specialties. From the spacious kitchen, through the dining and living area, and on out to the expansive deck, a dinner chez Bernard and Véronique is a movable feast.

Risotto aux Tomates et au Parmesan

RISOTTO WITH TOMATOES, SAFFRON, AND PARMESAN

Risotto is a dish that is extremely popular these days on French menus and in French homes, from Paris to the Mediterranean. Bernard's savory, aromatic version, graced with a dash of saffron, makes a festive appetizer or a bright accompaniment to seafood dishes such as baked fish or grilled scallops.

SERVES 6 AS AN APPETIZER OR AS A SIDE DISH

4 to 5 cups chicken stock

5 tablespoons unsalted butter

1 small onion, minced

2 cups uncooked Arborio rice

1/4 teaspoon gently crushed saffron threads

1/2 cup freshly grated Parmesan

2 large ripe tomatoes, quartered, seeded, and minced

Fine sea salt

Freshly ground black pepper

1 cup loosely packed baby arugula, preferably wild, for garnish (optional)

In a medium saucepan, bring the chicken stock to a simmer over medium heat. Reduce the heat and keep it at a very low simmer while you prepare the risotto.

In a large, heavy-bottomed saucepan, melt 3 tablespoons of the butter over medium heat. Add the onion, stir, and sauté until the onions are softened but not browned, about 3 minutes. Add the rice and stir to mix well, so that all the grains are coated. Add 1 cup of the hot stock and cook, stirring constantly, until the rice absorbs the stock. The mixture should be kept at a constant simmer. Continue cooking, adding the stock 1/2 to 1 cup at a time, stirring constantly after each addition, and letting the rice absorb each new portion of stock.

When there are two cups of stock remaining, add the saffron and stir to combine. Continue adding the stock to the rice, stirring constantly, until the rice is tender and creamy, but still a bit al dente. (You may not need to add all the chicken stock.) Add the Parmesan, tomatoes, and the remaining 2 tablespoons of butter, and fold gently into the mixture. Season to taste with salt and pepper. Serve immediately on warmed plates. Each serving may be garnished, if you wish, with a small handful of arugula.

SOURCE GUIDE

A Guide to French Country Kitchen Sources in France and the United States

In the course of researching this book, seeking out the best of all things authentically French relating to kitchens, kitchen design, and decoration, I came to know many sources for the kitchens and kitchen elements featured in these pages—dealers, designers, ateliers, markets, and shops. In this directory I offer an overview of sources, both in France and in the United States, for furniture, fabrics, faience, tiles, architectural salvage, cookware, tableware, and a broad range of decorative accessories. When calling France from the United States, dial 011-33, then drop the first 0 of the listed telephone number.

PHOTOGRAPH BY BEN SARLE

ANTIQUES

IN FRANCE

This listing of dealers barely scratches the surface of the French antiques world, but they are dealers we know and recommend. Several are featured in this book. For those visiting France, and who love the thrill of the hunt, there are flea markets or *brocante* fairs almost every day somewhere in the country, and you never know what you'll come upon. A fabulous set of hammered tin-copper-Bakelite canisters is one of my most treasured flea-market finds. A French publication, *Aladin* (www.aladinmag.com), available at kiosks and magazine shops in France, is aimed at devoted antiques lovers and buyers. It features an in-depth guide to all current and future antiques shows, fairs, shops, and markets. A French website, www.pointsdechine.com, offers a comprehensive (and easy-to-comprehend) listing of antique and *brocante* fairs, including addresses and dates, all over France. Wherever you travel, watch for "Brocante" signs or postings for "Vide-Greniers"—literally attic-emptiers—which are informal jumble sales. There is always the chance of scoring a rural find after sifting through the dross.

ANTIQUITÉS MAURIN
4, rue de Grille
13200 Arles
Tel.: 04-90-96-51-57
www.antiquites-maurin.com

A shop brimming with rare nineteenth-century Apt plates and platters and gilt-framed mirrors from Beaucaire, as well as quality regional furniture.

AU PETIT BONHEUR LA CHANCE
13, rue Saint-Paul
Paris 75004
Tel.: 01-42-74-36-38

A tiny shop full of charming kitchen collectibles—enamel coffeepots, canisters, linens, hot plates, porcelain, and much more.

BACHELIER ANTIQUITÉS
Marché Paul Bert (at the Paris Flea Market, Saint-Ouen), Allée 1, Stand 17
18, rue Paul Bert
93400 Saint-Ouen
Tel.: 01-40-11-89-98
www.bachelier-antiquites.com

An alluring shop (called a "stand" at the flea market) with a fantastic collection of old copper pots and molds, signs, lanterns, authentic butcher-block tables, antique stoves, linens, pottery, and utensils.

JEAN-JACQUES BOURGEOIS (MÉMOIRES D'UN ÂNE)
5, avenue des Quatre-Otages
84800 L'Isle-sur-la-Sorgue
Tel.: 04-90-20-63-15

Eighteenth- and nineteenth-century fauteuils and walnut commodes, charming paintings and engravings, vintage porcelain, and handmade reproductions commissioned from the shop's originals.

BRUNO CARLES
209-235, avenue de Lattre-de-Tassigny
34400 Lunel
Tel.: 04-67-71-36-10
www.brunocarles.fr

Antiques and Bruno's beautiful reproductions of regional Provençal chairs, commodes, bibliothèques, and tables in a variety of colors, each finished with at least six coats of paint for a handsome patina.

CUISINEOPHILE
28, rue Bourg-Tibourg
Paris 75004
Tel.: 01-40-29-07-32

A charming little shop in the Marais with intriguing antique kitchen elements and a lovely collection of ceramics.

DECO BISTRO
3, avenue du Clos Mouron
BP 68 71700 Tournus
Tel.: 03-85-32-10-52
E-mail: info@decobistro.com
www.decobistro.com

In Burgundy, Jean-Luc Perrier's emporium is really worth the visit if you love bistro, restaurant, and advertising collectibles. More than a just a store, it's an enclave of little shops—some re-creations of entire old bistros that feature bistro tables and chairs, posters, mirrors, and, most notably, fabulous old zinc and marble-topped bars.

F. DERVIEUX
5, rue Vernon
13200 Arles
Tel.: 04-90-96-02-39
www.dervieux.com

Antiques and reproductions; handsome furniture such as sculpted armoires, as well as smaller items, including a dainty walnut verrier (glassware cabinet). Beautiful reproductions made in an on-site atelier.

LA PETITE FADETTE
32, boulevard de la République
91450 Soisy-sur-Seine
Tel.: 01-64-57-90-97

A small, charming shop with both original and reproduction furniture and objets from the eighteenth and nineteenth centuries, as well as decorating accessories such as lamp shades and pillows.

LE MARQUIS DE CARABAS
Mesnil Girault
91690 Boissy-la-Rivière
Tel.: 01-64-94-88-57

Martine Ouvrard's lovely antiques enclave on an eighteenth-century farmhouse property, with well-priced eighteenth- and nineteenth-century furniture, some restored or "repatinated," as well as ornaments and furniture for the garden.

LE MAS DE CUREBOURG (HÉLÈNE DEGRUGILLIER-DAMPEINE)
Route d'Apt
84800 L'Isle-sur-la-Sorgue
Tel.: 04-90-20-30-06
www.mas-de-curebourg.com

A stone farmhouse emporium on the Route d'Apt, stocked with rustic eighteenth- and nineteenth-century painted armoires, vintage straw hats, and colorful regional pottery from Apt. Also an excellent line of reproductions.

MONLEAU
44, rue Nationale
30300 Vallabrègues
Tel.: 04-66-59-20-17

Period reproduction chairs and banquettes.

OBJETS EN TRANSIT
Marché Dauphine (at the Paris Flea Market, Saint-Ouen), Stand 122
140, rue des Rosiers
93400 Saint-Ouen
Tel.: 06-82-66-05-34
E-mail: contact@objetsentransit.com
www.objetsentransit.com

A treasure chest of bistro tables and chairs, vintage industrial storage and commercial lettering, artisan stools, architectural elements, and more.

IN THE UNITED STATES

COUNTRY LOFT ANTIQUES
557 Main Street South
Woodbury, CT 06798
Tel.: 203-266-4500
www.countryloftantiques.com

A dream of an antiques destination for anyone in the New York area, located in the hills of Woodbury, Connecticut, on the property known as the Samuel Bull Homestead. Carole Winer's emporium carries a wide variety of French country furniture, both antique and reproduction, as well as culinary antiques and wine-related collectibles. Here, displayed in historic barns, you'll find such items as farm and refectory tables, faience, armoires, buffets, baker's racks, wine racks, wine-tasting tables, copperware, antique stoves, and rush-seated chairs and benches.

ÎLE-DE-FRANCE ANTIQUES
289 Main Sreet South
Woodbury, CT 06798
   and
267 New Milford Turnpike, Route 202
Marbledale (Washington), CT 06777
Tel./Fax: 860-868-4321
E-mail:
Xavier@iledefranceantiques.com
www.iledefranceantiques.com

Two lovely, luminous shops in western Connecticut, specializing in culinary and wine-related antiques and vintage items—enchanting collections of enamel coffeepots, bars, clocks, signs, stoneware urns, rush-seated chairs, farm tables, copperware, and buffets à deux corps.

LES PIERRE ANTIQUES
369 Bleecker Street
New York, NY 10014
Tel.: 212-243-7740
E-mail: info@lespierreinc.com
www.lespierreinc.com

The sublime shop formerly known as Pierre Deux Antiques, the seminal French country shop founded by Pierre Moulin and Pierre Le Vec that ignited America's love for all things French country. Come here for beautifully crafted high-end eighteenth- and nineteenth-century antiques, such as rectangular farm tables and round dining tables in cherry, oak, and walnut; rush-seated banquette benches; butcher's tables; gorgeous armoires from Provence, Normandy, the Loire Valley, and the Île-de-France; chandeliers in tole, wrought iron, crystal, or wood; candlesticks; faience; porcelain; carriage lanterns; and pastoral prints and paintings.

MULLIN-JONES ANTIQUITIES
525 Main Street
Great Barrington, MA 01230
Tel.: 413-528-4871

One of my favorite shops in the Berkshires. Patrice Mullin offers an eclectic mix of French antique and vintage furniture and objects, from eighteenth-century provincial to sophisticated 1930s moderne. Among the trove here are mirrors, bistro tables, jelly cupboards, bucolic landscape paintings, and cushy, sensuously carved upholstered armchairs. Every room of her shop, in an antique New England farmhouse, offers a discovery. "I scramble everything up," she says of her whimsical rooms, "just like in a true French home."

ANTIQUE ARCHITECTURAL ELEMENTS • Period stonework,
antique tiles, a set of great old doors, vintage mantelpieces, and rustic, hand-carved sinks add wonderful character and charm to a house, whether it's an authentic Colonial farmhouse or a state-of-the-art creation of glass, steel, and redwood. Restored and unrestored architectural elements are in high demand throughout France. Below are some fine sources.

JEAN CHABAUD, LES MATÉRIAUX ANCIENS
21, route de Gargas
84400 Apt
Tel.: 04-90-74-07-61

Antique carved stone mantelpieces, garden statues, canal tiles, street signs, and stone fountains.

PORTES ANCIENNES/ANTIQUE DOORS
Route d'Avignon
13210 Saint-Rémy-de-Provence
Tel.: 04-90-92-13-13
www.portesanciennes.com

A wide selection of, not surprisingly, antique doors.

CHRISTIAN SEILLE, LES MILLES ET UNE PORTES
Place Émile-Zola
83570 Carcès
Tel.: 04-94-04-50-27

Antique doors of all sorts, perhaps even 1001, as well as vintage paneling, antique furniture, and bibelots.

ARTISTS • Among the artists
whose work appears in these pages are the two contemporary painters below.

CAROLE AKINS
The Studio
438 31st Street
Newport Beach, CA 92663
Tel.: 949-673-8663
www.caroleakins.com

DANIELLE MERCIER
Boisvieux
26210 Lapeyrouse
Tel.: 04-75-31-82-58

COOKWARE

A. SIMON
36, rue Étienne-Marcel
   and
48, rue Montmartre
75002 Paris
Tel.: 01-42-33-71-65
www.simon-a.com

One of the great professional restaurant supply houses in Paris, where home cooks as well as professional chefs come for their pots and pans, glassware, flatware, dishes, menu boards, and so much more.

BRIDGE KITCHENWARE
711 Third Avenue
New York, NY 10017
Tel.: 212-688-4220
www.bridgekitchenware.com

One of the best U.S. sources for imported kitchenware, Bridge has been supplying cookware, bakeware, pastry equipment, porcelain, kitchen appliances, and accessories for more than sixty years to restaurants, hotels, and home cooks.

DEHILLERIN
18-20, rue Coquillière
75001 Paris
Tel.: 01-42-36-53-13
www.e-dehillerin.fr

Since 1820, this legendary corner cookware shop in the old Les Halles area of Paris has been specializing in gorgeous copper pots and pans, selling both retail and wholesale to hotels and restaurants around the world—as well as to home cooks. Dehillerin is worth the trip just to see the displays of museum-quality wares. Even if you don't think you need anything new for your kitchen, you'll change your mind as soon as you step in the door.

ÉMILE HENRY
The Émile Henry Boutique in Marcigny Z.I. (factory store)
71110 Marcigny
Tel.: 03-85-25-50-70
www.emilehenry.com

Beautiful ceramic cooking vessels—gratin dishes, terrines, fluted flan dishes, ramekins, casseroles—that go from the oven directly to the table, as well as attractive glazed tableware. Émile Henry recently launched "Flame" a new line of stovetop ceramic cookers (stewpots, braisers, roasters, and tagine pots) designed for cooking directly on gas, electric, or halogen burners. Since they contain no metal, they can also be used in the microwave. The lines of these pots and dishes are sleek, the colors— charcoal, deep red, and mustard yellow— handsome; a nice addition to any French country kitchen.

LE CREUSET
902, rue Olivier Deguise
02230 Fresnoy-le-Grand
U.S. Tel.: 1-877-273-8738, ext. 6
www.lecreuset.com

Famous for their enameled cast-iron pots and casseroles that last for generations, the company also offers durable, nonporous stoneware with gleaming enameled surfaces, and practical, heat-resistant silicone bakeware and tools.

MAUVIEL (U.S. HEADQUARTERS)
802 Centerpoint Boulevard
New Castle, DE 12720
Tel.: 802-326-4803
www.mauviel.com

The Mauviel company, based in Normandy, has been creating high-quality lines of professional and home cookware for almost two hundred years. I love their stainless-steel-lined copper pots and pans, and their sturdy stainless-steel roasting pans with graceful cast-steel handles.

DECORATORS AND DESIGNERS • Below are a handful of top decorators and designers whose work distinguishes some of the finest and most charming homes in France, and French country-inspired homes in the United States.

HUGUES BOSC
Bosc Architecture
38, boulevard Victor-Hugo
13532 Saint-Rémy-de-Provence
Tel.: 04-90-92-10-81
E-mail: bosc.architecte@wanadoo.fr

MARIE-DOMINIQUE DE MONTMARIN
12, bis avenue de Verzy
75017 Paris
Tel.: 06-09-18-22-05

DAVID EASTON
David Easton Interiors
72 Spring Street
New York, NY 10012
Tel.: 212-334-3820
www.davideastoninc.com

PHILIPPE ECKERT
Mas de la Dame
Chemin Saint-Gabriel
13160 La Crau de Châteaurenard
Tel.: 04-32-62-10-45

CHARLES FAUDREE
1345 East 15th Street
Tulsa, OK 74120
Tel.: 918-747-9706
www.charlesfaudree.com

JACQUES GARCIA
212, rue de Rivoli
75001 Paris
Tel.: 01-49-97-48-70

NONO GIRARD
La Capucine Décoration
86, allée Jean-Jaurès
84200 Carpentras
Tel.: 04-90-60-36-58

PATRICE NOURISSAT
94, rue Amelot
75011 Paris
Tel.: 01-47-97-27-47

MARIE-JOSÉ POMMEREAU
Barocco
14, rue Clément-Marot
75008 Paris
Tel.: 06-11-47-11-00

ESTELLE RÉALE
Villa Estelle
5, montée de la Bourgade
86800 Hauts-de-Cagnes
Tel.: 04-92-02-89-83

ALINE STEINBACH
Chateau de Ceris
84220 Luoux
Tel.: 04-90-75-04-16
asteinbach@orange.fr

CAROLE WINER
557 Main Street South
Woodbury, CT 06798
Tel.: 203-266-4500
www.countryloftantiques.com

FABRICS • The French country kitchens featured in these pages are vibrant, with distinctive fabrics sourced from a variety of producers and shops. Below are contacts for many of them.

TRADITIONAL FABRIC HOUSES

MANUEL CANOVAS
12-23 Grosvenor Hill
London W1K 3QD
United Kingdom
Tel.: 020-731-86000
www.manuelcanovas.com

PIERRE FREY
27, rue du Mail
75002 Paris
Tel.: 02-44-77-36-00
  and
1 and 2, rue de Furstenberg
75006 Paris
Tel.: 01-46-33-73-00
www.pierrefrey.com

LES INDIENNES DE NÎMES (TISSUS LE MISTRAL)
2, boulevard des Arènes
30000 Nîmes
Tel.: 04-66-83-49-16
www.indiennesdenimes.fr

LES OLIVADES
Chemin des Indienneurs
13103 Saint-Étienne-du-Grès (and boutiques throughout France)
Tel.: 04-90-49-19-19
www.lesolivades.com

SPECIALTY FABRIC BOUTIQUES

ÉDITH MÉZARD
Chemin de l'Ange
84200 Lumières (Goult)
Tel.: 04-90-72-36-41

Exquisite hand-embroidered table linens.

LA MAISON BIEHN
7, rue des Quatre-Otages,
84800 L'Isle-sur-la-Sorgue
Tel.: 04-90-20-89-04

A wonderful collection of antique Provençal fabrics, antique quilts, and rustic contemporary linens.

LE RIDEAU DE PARIS
32, rue du Bac
75007 Paris
Tel.: 01-42-61-18-56

Florence Maeght produces fine reproductions of her collections of eighteenth- and nineteenth-century textiles and quilts—bed quilts, tablecloths, place mats, handbags, and more. Unique aprons, pillows, curtains, tablecloths, and bibs from antique textiles by Françoise Méchin-Pellet; also contemporary ready-to-wear from lush, modern textiles.

PIERRE DEUX
Stores nationwide.
Tel.: 888-743-7732
www.pierredeux.com

In their many shops around the United States, with headquarters in New York, Pierre Deux offers a lavish array of French fabrics, including tapestries, geometrics, floral prints, jacquards, and especially gorgeous toiles in a delectable variety of colorations.

FAIENCE, POTTERY • The following firms produce faience and pottery from great terra-cotta urns to marbled-clay dinnerware to whimsically patterned plates and platters.

ANTONY PITOT
Quartier de Ponty, Route Nationale 100
84220 Goult
Tel.: 04-90-72-22-79

Fine yellow and green faience in the eighteenth-century Apt tradition.

ASTIER DE VILLATTE
173, rue Saint-Honoré
75001 Paris
Tel.: 01-42-60-74-13
www.astierdevillatte.com *and*
www.collection-regards.com

Here is the original source for beautiful eighteenth-century-inspired white-glazed plates, platters, teapots, candlesticks, and bowls, widely seen in knockoffs produced by chain stores. The originals, created by Jean-Baptiste Astier de Villatte in the Loire town of Chinon, have a very distinctive look that results from dark clays glazed with white enamels. Many pieces have handcrafted relief patterns.

ATELIER DU VIEIL APT
61, place Carnot
84400 Apt
Tel.: 04-90-04-03-96
www.atelierduvieilapt.com

In the tradition of the late faiencier *Jean Faucon, whose grandfather resurrected an eighteenth-century Apt style of marbled-clay faience in the early 1900s, the artisans here create exquisite and unique bowls, plates, platters, vases, and pitchers in marbled blue or brown clays under a clear glaze.*

ATELIER SOLEIL
Chemin Marcel-Provence and Chemin Quinson
04360 Moustiers-Sainte-Marie
Tel.: 04-92-74-63-05
www.soleil-deux.com

Traditional Moustiers faience, white glaze over red clay, and polychrome décors of flowers, Revolutionary motifs, and grotesques.

POTERIE DE HAUTE PROVENCE
Route de Nyons
26220 Dieulefit
Tel.: 04-75-46-42-10

Rustic glazed pots and dinnerware from a traditional and picturesque pottery village.

POTERIE RAVEL
Avenue des Goums
13400 Aubagne
Tel.: 04-42-18-79-79
www.poterie-ravel.com

A venerable family company producing large unglazed terra-cotta planters as well as glazed yellow and green dinnerware for more than a hundred years

VÉRONIQUE PICHON
19, bis avenue de la Gare
30700 Uzès

Continuing the long tradition of Pichon faience in elegant, often art deco or turn-of-the-century designs.

FURNITURE • While authentic French country antiques are becoming more and more difficult to find, even in France, high-quality French-inspired reproduction furniture is increasingly available, made from fine woods and lovingly handcrafted. Styles and authenticity of line and finish do vary, however. The following producers and merchants offer items worth considering if you want attractive French style without the effort to obtain originals, and without the high price tags.

AUFFRANCE CO., INC.
Tel.: 212-371-9665
www.auffrance.com

BAKER FURNITURE
Jacques Garcia Collection
Tel.: 800-592-2537
www.bakerfurniture.com

CENTURY FURNITURE
Tel.: 800-852-5552
www.centuryfurniture.com

DREXEL HERITAGE
Accents Français and Accents Provence collections
www.drexelheritage.com

FRENCH HERITAGE
Maison du Soleil and Avenue Montaigne Collections
Tel.: 800-245-0899
www.frenchheritage.com

THE FRENCH TRADITION CABINETRY
Tel.: 310-719-9977
www.thefrenchtradition.com

PIERRE DEUX
Tel.: 888-743-7732
www.pierredeux.com

RANGES AND STOVES • Many of the dazzling kitchens featured in these pages have as a centerpiece a glorious, often custom-made, kitchen range from La Cornue or Lacanche. These two producers have cornered the market for upscale, state-of-the-art ranges with incomparable vintage allure. The La Cornue ranges, often called "the Rolls-Royce of kitchen ranges," are handcrafted in France, as they have been since 1908, out of cast iron, steel, solid brass, nickel, and enamel. Produced by a team of only sixty artisans, most of these ranges are built to order, and there is a wait of at least two months. The Lacanche ranges are also made to order at a factory in the Côte d'Or area of Burgundy that has its roots in a nineteenth-century ironworks. Most La Cornue and Lacanche ranges offer both gas and electric cooking options.

LACANCHE
www.lacanche.com

U.S. distributor:
Art Culinaire, Lacanche USA
17721 132nd Avenue NE
Woodinville, WA 98072
Tel.: 800-570-2433
E-mail: sales@frenchranges.com
www.lacancheusa.com

LA CORNUE
www.lacornue.com

U.S. distributor:
Purcell Murray Inc.
185 Park Lane
Brisbane, CA 94005
Tel.: 800-892-4040
www.purcellmurray.com

TILE PRODUCERS AND PURVEYORS

THE ANTIQUE FLOOR COMPANY
Philip Marr
Hameau Dracy Chalas
21230 Vievy
Tel.: 03-80-90-50-62
www.theantiquefloorcompany.com

Charming Englishman Philip Marr, a Francophile living in Burgundy, scours the countryside buying up vintage tile flooring, primarily late-nineteenth- and early-twentieth-century cement tiles, from crumbling farmhouses and dusty cellars throughout the countryside. He sells complete floors to clients in France as well as in the United States. Homes in Atlanta, Chicago, Los Angeles, Seattle, and Silver City, New Mexico, among other locales, are newly resplendent with antique cement tile floors in their kitchens and dining rooms, all sourced by Philip.

ATELIER ALAIN VAGH
Route d'Entrecasteaux,
83630 Salernes
Tel.: 04-94-70-61-85

One of the best artisans in this famous village of tile makers, with plain and patterned tiles in traditional and contemporary designs.

CAROCIM
1515, route du Pur-Sainte-Rapide
13540 Puyricard
Tel.: 04-42-92-20-39
www.carocim.com

Carocim, located near Aix-en-Provence, is the source for beautifully hued, batch-dyed cement tiles, some with a matte finish, some with a soft sheen. They produce a wide variety of patterns, nineteenth-century vintage designs, styles based on Souleido fabric motifs, geometrics, and more, as well as solid colors.

DIDIER GRUEL
Le Grand Montagne, Chemin du Lozet
30400 Villeneuve-lès-Avignon
Tel.: 04-90-25-08-07

Gruel, located high in the hills just outside Avignon, is a specialist in beautiful old cement tiles. Call for an appointment.

JOSSE
33, route de Dinard
22130 Plancoët
Tel.: 02-96-84-03-40
www.jossefrance.com

On the northern coast of Brittany, Josse is renowned for its production of stunning cement tiles—more than thirty styles in their Décors line—in classic late-nineteenth-century and early-twentieth-century designs. They also produce an elegant terra-cotta line of blue-and-white tiles; the Fleur-de-Lis, Bretagne, and Vieille France patterns are among my favorites.

MESGUICH MOSAIK GALLERY
459 Washington Street
New York, NY 10013
Tel.: 212-226-8218
www.mesguichmosaik.co.uk

Pierre Mesguich, whose kitchen is featured on pages 90–97, shows his work and designs for clients at this gallery in downtown New York City, the U.S. outpost of his mosaic empire headquartered in London.

VERNIN CARREAUX D'APT
Route Nationale 100
84480 Bonnieux
Tel.: 04-90-04-63-04
www.carreaux-d-apt.com

Dazzling handmade, hand-painted glazed tiles in 165 gorgeous colors; custom patterns of your choice to order.

VACATION RENTALS • I spend

many weeks a year in France, and my favorite form of lodging is a cozy, stylish rental, either an apartment in Paris or a small house in Provence. Many people ask me how I find my "homes away from home," so I'm happy to share some of my sources.

CHEZ VOUS
1001 Bridgeway, PMB 245
Sausalito, CA 94965
Tel.: 415-331-2535
www.chezvous.com

In Paris I love the agency Chez Vous, run by Sharyl and Paul Rupert, lifelong Francophiles from Sausalito who started their Paris apartment business as a labor

of love. Today they have more than forty properties, each carefully vetted and usually renovated with new kitchens and bathrooms, new bedding, and a fresh décor. They rent for a minimum of five days. I've booked five or six different apartments through Chez Vous, usually on the Left Bank, and have had a wonderful stay in each. Chez Vous has a beguiling, user-friendly website where you can take a virtual visit of each apartment.

ÉMILE GARCIN
3, rue de l'Université
75007 Paris
Tel.: 01-42-61-73-38
www.emilegarcin.com

Garcin and his team are the source for beautiful, high-end rentals and sales in Paris, the Île-de-France region, and Provence. Come here for your château, your antique watermill, your manoir, your Provençal farmhouse, your private mansion in the Marais, or your pied-à-terre on the Ile-Saint-Louis. Rentals are generally for a month or more.

LUBERON INVESTISSEMENTS
La Combe
84220 Gordes
Tel.: 04-90-72-07-55
www.lubinvest.com

Agent extraordinaire and man-about-Provence Vincent Boeuf and his large team offer high-quality, mostly luxe rentals throughout the Luberon, as well as in Aix-en-Provence, Fontvieille, Lourmarin, Manosque, Saint-Saturnin d'Apt, and other locations. The agency is also a renowned real estate firm selling many of the region's most sought-after properties. His clientele spans the globe from Hong Kong to Brunei to Hollywood to Paris.

INDEX

RECIPE INDEX

LISTED BY APPEARANCE IN BOOK